Resolving Problems and Conflicts

Agency for Instructional Technology

SOUTH-WESTERN
—★—
THOMSON LEARNING

Australia • Canada • Mexico • Singapore • Spain • United Kingdom • United States

SOUTH-WESTERN
™
THOMSON LEARNING

Communication 2000, 2E: **Resolving Problems and Conflicts**
by Agency for Instructional Technology

Editor-in-Chief:
Jack Calhoun

**Vice President/
Executive Publisher:**
Dave Shaut

Team Leader:
Karen Schmohe

Executive Editor:
Eve Lewis

Project Manager:
Laurie Wendell

**Executive Marketing
Manager:**
Carol Volz

Channel Manager:
Nancy A. Long

Marketing Coordinator:
Linda Kuper

Production Editor:
Alan Biondi

Production Manager:
Patricia Matthews Boies

Technology Editor:
Matthew McKinney

**Manufacturing
Coordinator:**
Kevin Kluck

**Developer and
Compositor:**
Agency for Instructional
Technology

CD-ROM Developer:
Vandalay Group, Inc.

Printer:
Quebecor World
Dubuque, Iowa

**Illustration, Cover and
Internal Design:**
Tippy McIntosh

ISBN: 0-538-43331-0

HOW TO USE THIS BOOK

The updated *Communication 2000* is a multimedia communication skills series that prepares learners to meet the communication challenges of tomorrow's workplace. Twelve modules provide comprehensive coverage of workplace communication skills, along with numerous opportunities for critical thinking, project-based activities, and technology applications.

Resolving Problems and Conflicts delves into strategies for resolving differences and understanding coworkers' points of view. Learn methods for resolving workplace conflicts, including active listening, negotiation, prevention, and serving as a peacemaker.

The following page illustrations identify key features of this guide.

WORKSHOPS

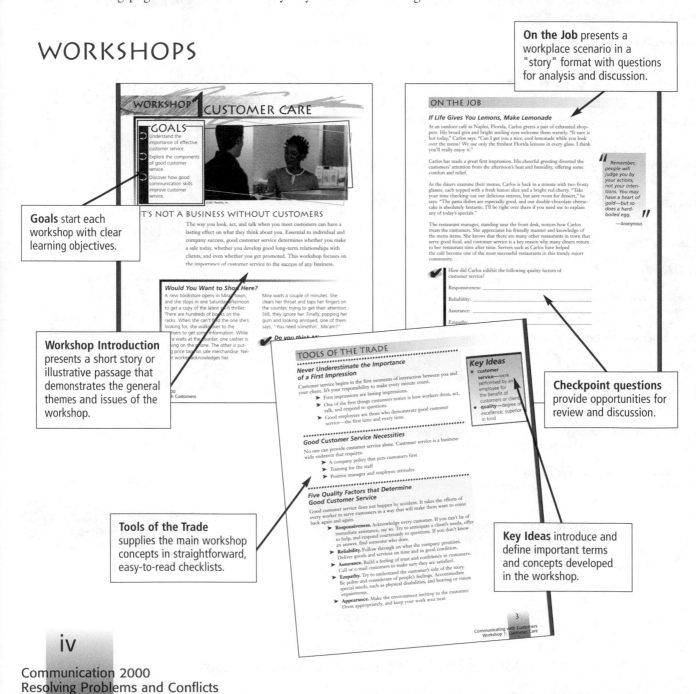

On the Job presents a workplace scenario in a "story" format with questions for analysis and discussion.

Goals start each workshop with clear learning objectives.

Workshop Introduction presents a short story or illustrative passage that demonstrates the general themes and issues of the workshop.

Tools of the Trade supplies the main workshop concepts in straightforward, easy-to-read checklists.

Checkpoint questions provide opportunities for review and discussion.

Key Ideas introduce and define important terms and concepts developed in the workshop.

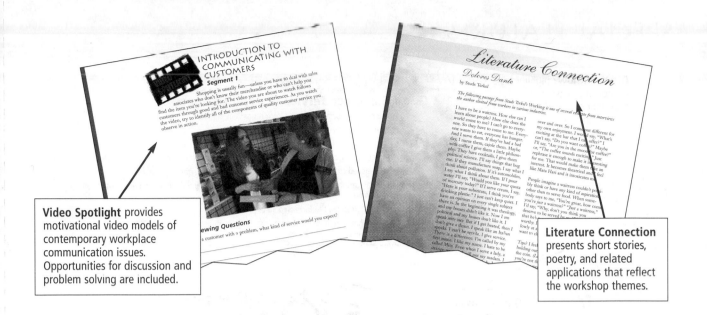

Video Spotlight provides motivational video models of contemporary workplace communication issues. Opportunities for discussion and problem solving are included.

Literature Connection presents short stories, poetry, and related applications that reflect the workshop themes.

REVIEW AND ASSESSMENT

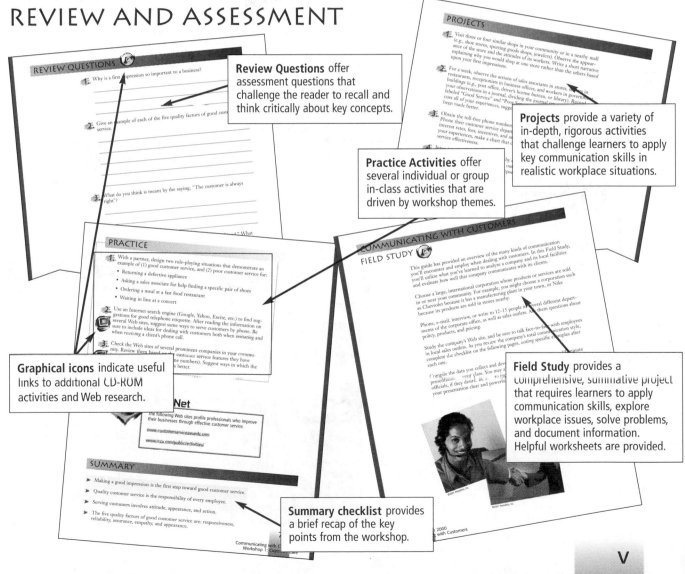

Review Questions offer assessment questions that challenge the reader to recall and think critically about key concepts.

Projects provide a variety of in-depth, rigorous activities that challenge learners to apply key communication skills in realistic workplace situations.

Practice Activities offer several individual or group in-class activities that are driven by workshop themes.

Graphical icons indicate useful links to additional CD-ROM activities and Web research.

Field Study provides a comprehensive, summative project that requires learners to apply communication skills, explore workplace issues, solve problems, and document information. Helpful worksheets are provided.

Summary checklist provides a brief recap of the key points from the workshop.

SPECIAL FEATURES

Did You Know? highlights interesting facts, findings, and trends in workplace communication.

DID YOU KNOW?

Good Customer Service Is Good Business

◇ 65% of a company's business comes from repeat customers.
◇ Customers refer friends, who then become customers.
◇ Unhappy customers tell 8–16 people about their bad experiences.
◇ Through Internet chat rooms, an unhappy customer can now tell thousands of people!
◇ 91% of dissatisfied customers won't shop at the same store again.
◇ A company can increase profits from 25% to 100% by simply reducing the number of unhappy customers.
◇ Customer loyalty can lead to increased sales.
◇ If a problem is handled quickly and to a customer's complete satisfaction, 80% will do business with the company again.

> *Remember, people will judge you by your actions, not your intentions. You may have a heart of gold—but so does a hard-boiled egg.*
>
> —Anonymous

Quotations add relevance, humor, and motivational messages.

On the Net

The following Web sites profile professionals who improve their businesses through effective customer service.

www.customerserviceawards.com

www.icsa.com/public/activities/

On the Net links communication skills to Web research and online learning through suggested Web sites and activities.

World View provides international and multicultural examples of key workshop concepts.

Not Quite/Got It Right presents contrasting good and poor examples of communication skills.

WORLD VIEW

Simple conventions or practices that are natural to you may be offensive to people in other countries. The following list describes just a few.

Morocco	Holding a glass in your left hand
Germany	Being even a few minutes late for an appointment
Saudi Arabia	Wearing shorts, even for casual dress
Japan	Singling an employee out for a compliment

⊘ Not Quite

... a customer service representative for a ...ful sporting goods supplier. At least half of ...y is spent negotiating with clients on the phone.

...e he was eating lunch at his desk, Luke let the phone ring several times, ...ller would go away. He finally picked up the phone and addressed the caller, who wanted to learn more about his company's products. Interested only in his lunch, Luke told the man that he would get back to him soon.

Two weeks passed. Luke never returned that call, but he did find out who it was—one of the biggest sporting goods retailers. When their call was never returned, they chose a competing supplier instead.

✓ Got It Right

As a secretary in a large construction firm, Akiko spends almost her entire day answering calls from clients, salespeople, and inspectors. It is not uncommon for her to have three or four calls coming in at one time.

When that happens, Akiko has to prioritize the most important calls. She may put three people on hold at once, but always asks for their permission first, and never leaves them on hold longer than 40 seconds. If she is not able to talk with them, she will politely take their names and numbers and call them back as soon as possible. Akiko lets no call go unanswered, which her firm's contacts greatly appreciate.

Ethics & Etiquette requires readers to think critically about an ethical dilemma or difficult situation.

Ethics & Etiquette

What do you do when a customer cannot afford your product but you know a competitor who sells it at a cheaper price? Should you tell the customer, discount your product, or simply say nothing?

CREDITS

Agency for Instructional Technology

Print and Media Production
Instructional Designer
Dr. Richard Lookatch

Senior Editor
Lesa Petersen

Assistant Editor
Catherine Riley

Print Design and Composition
Karla Dunn
David Strange

Features Writer
Daniel J. Crowley

Writers
Sheryl Szot Gallaher
Stephanie H. Zaiser
Dr. Mark Doremus
Sandra Lookatch
Vandalay Group, Inc.

Permissions
Brad Bloom
Nicole Griffin

CD-ROM and WebTutor Production
Vandalay Group, Inc.

ExamView Test Bank Writer
Dr. Mark Doremus

Video Production
Producer
Dr. David Gudaitis

Associate Producer
Jill E. Turner

Video Script Writer
Bob Risher

Video Editor
Martin O'Neill

Animation and Graphics
Bill Crawford

Assistant Video Editor
Laura Crouch

Stock Footage
Brad Bloom

Communication 2000 *Reviewers*

Anna Cook
Education and Workplace Literacy Consultant
Austin, TX

Tony Hoess
Marketing Teacher
Pendleton, KY

Carol S. Jackson
English Teacher and Technology Teacher Leader
Irmo, SC

Kay Orrell
Business Education Resource Consortium
   Project Manager
Santa Maria, CA

Nicola Pidgeon
Coordinator of Workforce Development
Schenectady, NY

Brian Sporleder
Dean of Instruction
Milwaukee, WI

CONTENTS

©2001 PhotoDisc, Inc.

©2001 PhotoDisc, Inc.

GOALS

⟳ Understand the role of perception in conflict.

⟳ Discover and utilize strategies for understanding someone else's point of view.

©2001 PhotoDisc, Inc.

WALKING IN YOUR COWORKERS' SHOES

It's probably impossible to truly "walk in someone else's shoes"—to know, understand, and feel what another person has experienced. No one can completely understand what it is like, for example, to be a member of a different ethnic group—the unfairness suffered, or the special sense of community. Though we can't really walk in someone else's shoes, respecting and considering the perspectives that might lie behind another person's words and actions is essential for avoiding misunderstandings. Seeing both sides of a conflict is the only way to reach acceptable solutions. This workshop demonstrates how perspective influences conflicts and conflict resolution—in the workplace, and in life.

Who's at Fault?

Michael: Someday I'm going to have it out with Orlando in the mail room!

Sasha: Orlando? Why?

Michael: Last Friday at 4:30 I dropped a stack of outgoing mail from my department on the counter. All I said was, 'Have a nice weekend,' and he snarled at me.

Sasha: Mike, he probably thought you were being sarcastic. You dumped a load of work on him at the end of the day and then wished him a nice weekend—it sounds like a bad joke.

 Was Michael justified in being angry with Orlando?

TOOLS OF THE TRADE

Seeing the Other Side

In conflict, emotions run high. The words and actions of others can seem doubly misguided and even hurtful when we are trying to express something we want or believe in. When involved in misunderstandings and conflicts, it is important to remember that the other person is not trying to hinder your objectives, but is expressing his or her wants and beliefs, just like you. The following tips will help you to see both sides of any conflict.

➤ **Respect different worldviews.** Remember that everyone has a unique worldview based upon diverse life experiences. Listen in a way that acknowledges how the other person developed his or her worldview.

➤ **Let go of being "right."** Putting your opinions, beliefs, and values at risk is the scariest part of conflict. When you stop trying to convince the other person of your "rightness," your convictions are no longer "on the line"—freeing you to establish a common understanding.

➤ **Show empathy.** It is difficult to understand what anyone else is saying when your defenses are up. Instead of placing or accepting blame, listen empathetically—express care, understanding, and concern for the other person's position.

➤ **Don't react to communication styles.** Like perspectives, communication styles come in many shapes and sizes. Keep an open mind about unfamiliar communication styles, and understand that one style is not necessarily better than another. Ignore biting comments and tone of voice, and focus on the essence and content of the message.

➤ **Don't assume that you know what the other party wants.** A large percentage of misunderstandings stem from incorrect assumptions about the other party's goals and wishes.

Key Ideas

★ **perspective**— a particular evaluation of a situation or facts, especially from one person's point of view

★ **belief**—a conviction that certain things are true or real; confidence; faith; trust; an opinion

★ **worldview**— a personal interpretation or image of the universe and humanity; view of life

★ **empathy**—the ability to identify with and understand another person's feelings or difficulties

> *Sometimes I think that the main obstacle to empathy is our persistent belief that everybody is exactly like us.*
>
> —John Powell,
> geologist and ethnologist

INTRODUCTION TO CONFLICT IN THE WORKPLACE
Segment 1

This video segment focuses on the value of seeing the other side's perspective when resolving conflicts in the workplace. Experts on conflict resolution will talk about the finer points of listening, negotiation, and peacemaking. Examples of conflicts on the job will convey the importance of reaching win-win solutions. As you watch the video, think about the role that listening plays in avoiding and resolving workplace conflicts.

Respecting and considering your coworkers' perspectives is essential for avoiding conflict.

Post-Viewing Questions

1. Why is listening important for resolving conflicts?

_____

_____

2. How can understanding an opposing point of view help resolve conflicts?

_____

_____

3. What is wrong with a win-lose resolution?

_____

_____

ON THE JOB

Tough Times

Tim nervously glances out the window as the last employee takes a seat in his office. He clears his throat and begins.

Tim: You may have heard some rumors in the last week or so. Let me reassure you that there are no planned layoffs. However, because the company is going through tough times right now, we do need to increase our sales by 15 percent in the next three months.

Vera: But how can we do that? We're already putting in extra time just to maintain last year's sales level. What are you doing? How about putting in extra hours or getting out there on the sales floor?

Tim: Excuse me? I've been working night and day in meetings with the other managers to figure out how we can get through this without asking more of you, and this is the thanks I get?

Aiesha: Why should we thank you when we have to work twice as hard? We're doing our part.

Tim: Are you really trying hard enough? When I was on the sales floor, we cleared 300 units minimum each month—with fewer staff. We did it, and so can you, if you pick up the pace.

Vera: Things have changed since you were in sales. If you spent any time out there, you'd know there are fewer customers, and they're buying less. Give us some credit, will you?

Tim: Oh, come on, things haven't changed that much. You just need to get in there and sell more, that's all. *(Tim glances at his watch and continues.)* We can talk about this later. Think about what I said—and get to work!

 What is the problem? How does Tim see the problem? What might be influencing his point of view? How do his employees see the problem? What might be influencing their outlook? What would you suggest Tim and his employees do to help ease the problem?

_____

_____

_____

_____

> " *I never take my own side in a quarrel.*
>
> —Robert Frost, poet

5

1. Describe a conflict you've seen recently in a movie or television show from two different characters' points of view. Discuss how the resolution of the story would affect each character's perspective.

2. Divide into small groups and choose one of the topics below. Design short skits demonstrating miscommunication due to perception differences, and good communication that includes each side's point of view. Perform the skits for the class, and have the class evaluate the characters' conflict resolution skills.

   • Returning a damaged jacket to a store

   • Being late for work

   • Finding a location for the annual company party

3. 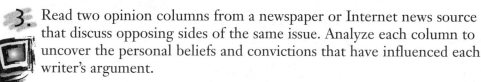 Read two opinion columns from a newspaper or Internet news source that discuss opposing sides of the same issue. Analyze each column to uncover the personal beliefs and convictions that have influenced each writer's argument.

4. Becoming sensitive to individual differences and learning to understand others' viewpoints is important in many different career fields. To sell a product, for example, you have to know what your customers need and want. On a separate piece of paper, briefly describe how this sensitivity could be useful in your desired career field.

SUMMARY

➤ When involved in misunderstandings and conflicts, it is important to remember that the other person is not trying to hinder your objectives, but is expressing his or her wants and beliefs, just like you.

➤ Trying to see both sides of a conflict is the only way to reach acceptable compromises and solutions.

> *Understand-
> ing is a two-way
> street.*
>
> —Eleanor
> Roosevelt

6

REVIEW QUESTIONS

1. What does "walking in someone else's shoes" mean?

_____

_____

_____

2. Name and describe a good strategy for understanding another person's point of view.

_____

_____

_____

PROJECTS

1. Identify a friend or family member and record your perception of their responsibilities and roles in life. Arrange a time when you can "change places" with them and "walk in their shoes." Record your activities and your feelings after the exchange. Include any changes in your perceptions of their role.

2. Think about the most irritating person you know, someone who disagrees with you on almost every issue. Suppose you wake up one morning and discover that you have become that person. What would be important to you? What would your major concerns be? What would the "new you" say about the person you were yesterday? Describe how the world appears to you from your new point of view.

3. As any actor can tell you, learning to "walk in someone else's shoes" isn't always easy. Actors must learn to feel, think, and speak like their characters. How do actors learn to do this? Talk with a drama instructor in your school, or with someone who performs with a theater group in your community. Adapt what you learn about acting to understanding someone else's perspective. Summarize what you learn in a brief instruction sheet for your class.

4. View three television programs that feature stories about workplaces. List all of the office conflicts that arise from perception differences. Describe how resolutions were attained in each circumstance.

GOALS

→ Identify different types of decisions and decision-making strategies.

→ Discover the importance of seeking common goals to solve problems.

→ Learn to separate symptoms and problems.

©2001 PhotoDisc, Inc.

DECISIONS, DECISIONS

We make decisions from the time we get out of bed in the morning to the time we return to bed at night. What to wear, where to go for lunch, who to hire for a position, when to schedule a meeting, how to solve a dispute between employees—the list goes on. This workshop focuses on problem solving and decision making in the workplace, provides decision-making techniques, and defines the roles that people and change play in solving problems and making decisions.

Happy Birthday Qui . . .

"I ran out of frosting!" Katie says panicked, overwhelmed with her preparations for her son Quincey's birthday party. "I need another tube of the silver frosting, or this cake will say Happy Birthday Qui!"

Katie sends her husband Tim to the grocery store. He stares at the frosting aisle, and immediately goes blank. "Was it white? Silver? Gold? The kind in the tube or the kind in the can? The kids will be there in 20 minutes!" Knowing time is of the essence, Tim buys a ready-made cake at the grocer's bakery.

When Tim returns with the bakery cake, Katie is astonished.

 What else could Tim have done to solve the problem?

TOOLS OF THE TRADE

Types of Decisions

Considering the timeline or deadline for a particular problem or question is an effective way to categorize and manage decisions. Three basic types of decisions, based on time needed for resolution, follow.

➤ **Long-range decisions.** Decisions that take years to make are generally the most risky.

Should the company move to another city?

➤ **Medium-range decisions.** Decisions that pertain to events over a period of a month or two are less risky and generally support your long-range decisions.

Should the current building lease be renewed for one or two years?

➤ **Short-range decisions.** Everyday decisions support medium-range decisions and are generally the least risky.

Should new letterhead showing the current address be reordered?

The Decision-Making "Wheel"

There are always decisions to be made—it is a lifelong process. Think of the following decision-making steps as spokes in a wheel that never stops turning.

➤ Recognize a decision-making opportunity or a problem.

➤ Gather all relevant information.

➤ Choose a strategy for solving the problem.

➤ Implement the solution.

➤ Begin the next decision-making opportunity.

The Problem-Solving Roles

Your value to an employer increases substantially when you can put current problems in the context of a bigger picture. The types of problem solvers follow. Though employers prefer proactive thinkers, most people are reactive.

➤ **Proactive.** Proactive people try to predict and prevent problems before they happen. They mold events to fit the future they desire. When problems arise, they think about the big picture, and seek long-term—not rash—solutions.

➤ **Reactive.** When problems occur, reactive people try to stabilize events or circumstances to sustain the least amount of harm. Reactive people don't think about problems until they happen. They react to a crisis without looking at how it influences the future.

➤ **No-action.** These people are not problem solvers. They go with the flow—they neither react to crises nor look to the future.

Key Ideas

★ **decision**— something that is chosen or determined after considering possible alternatives

★ **proactive**— taking the initiative by acting rather than reacting to events

★ **reactive**— reacting to events, situations, and stimuli, especially doing so spontaneously as they occur

★ **problem**—a difficult situation, matter, or person; a question or puzzle that needs to be solved

★ **symptom**—an indication of a disorder or problem

Separating Symptoms and Problems

In order to identify and ultimately solve a problem, you must deeply analyze the situation. Knowing how to distinguish symptoms from problems is a key part of this type of assessment. For example, a fever might be an indication of an infection, but if you simply take aspirin to control the fever (the symptom), you will not cure the infection (the problem). The following table gives some examples of treating symptoms versus treating problems.

TREATING A SYMPTOM	TREATING A PROBLEM
Digging paper out of the copier every time it jams.	Discovering that the company is using the wrong type of paper for the copier.
Decreasing employee lunch hours because productivity is down.	Assessing and treating the low morale problem that has created the decreased productivity.

Seeking Common Goals

According to the American Society for Training and Development and the U.S. Department of Labor, an organization's ability to achieve its goals depends on the problem-solving skills of its workforce. When solving a problem depends on the joint efforts of a team, the first step is to establish common goals.

Coworkers who set common goals:

➤ **See a purpose, not just a problem.** When employees work together to find a common goal, the focus shifts from correcting a problem to achieving a sense of purpose and meaning through a shared cause. When deciding on a common goal, coworkers should explore major opportunities, major problems, and potential threats to the team.

➤ **Create a sense of ownership.** When a decision is imposed on a team without the input of all involved, people are not likely to give their best. A sense of "ownership" of the problem and the higher goal will influence employees to "go the extra mile."

➤ **Focus on the team's effectiveness.** The "best" decision or solution to a problem is not truly going to be the best if the majority of the team is not in agreement. Sometimes, it is better to choose a "lower-quality" decision that is accepted by all. Otherwise, overall effectiveness will be poor.

Each problem that I solved became a rule, which served afterwards to solve other problems.

—Rene Descartes, philosopher

Decision-Making Strategies

Often, people do not carefully analyze problems before making decisions. Making a decision without appropriate consideration of all factors involved can lead to backtracking, lost time, and wasted resources. Simple T-charts and Decision Value charts will help you to solve the most complex problems.

USING A T-CHART
A T-chart is a simple graphic that shows the alternatives to consider when you need to make a decision.

➤ T-charts force people to look at pros and cons.

➤ T-charts reduce the risk of making ill-informed decisions based on too few facts.

T-Chart Example
Scott needs to decide whether to hire college students for a six-month research project.

PROS	CONS
• Available now	• Training required
• Low daily pay rate	• Competing priorities between work and school
• Long-term employment not needed	
• No employment benefits required	• Schedule conflicts
	• Lack of loyalty common in temporary workers

USING A DECISION VALUE CHART
A Decision Value chart visually organizes each option, the criteria for each option, and an assigned value for each criteria. A scale of 1 to 10 or any other measure can be used.

➤ Decision Value charts neatly organize multiple alternatives and decision-making factors.

➤ If you're honest about the values assigned, the choice will be clear.

Decision Value Chart Example
Jill is a travel agent who has been asked to organize a corporate planning retreat.

CRITERIA	Possible Points	Jamaica	Canada	Fishing	Staying Home
EXCITEMENT	25	25	15	10	0
RELAXATION	25	25	20	20	20
SCENERY	25	25	25	20	0
EASE OF ACCESS	25	10	20	20	25
TOTAL POINTS	100	85	80	70	45

Using Change to Your Advantage

The workplace is a hotbed of change. On any given day, your supervisor, responsibilities, and even your job title could change. Use the strategies below to make change an advantage instead of a problem.

➤ Utilize changed conditions to create new or improved ideas.

➤ Eliminate irrelevant or outdated processes when change allows.

➤ Improve lines of communication by developing brainstorming or discussion groups to evaluate the changes.

➤ Reassign priorities to match the changed conditions.

➤ Reassign personnel for greater efficiency.

➤ Think positively. If you consider change to be good, you'll see how change can present better solutions.

➤ Be flexible and creative.

➤ Juggle priorities. Today's problem may become unimportant tomorrow when another problem becomes critical.

➤ Accept some change, and accept what you cannot change. Fighting change can leave you frustrated and drained.

" In every success story, you can find someone who has made a courageous decision. "

—Peter F. Drucker, author

©2001 PhotoDisc, Inc.

Your value to an employer increases substantially when you can put current problems in the context of a bigger picture.

HOUSTON, WE HAVE A PROBLEM

You can make decisions based on hunches and guesswork, but the risk is greater when you do. The best decisions are carefully reasoned after all available information has been reviewed.

✔ Imagine you work in the marketing department for Houston's Swimming Pools. You've been asked to choose the entertainment for the outdoor grand opening. Your manager gives you three possible bands and a fact sheet on each. Fill in the Decision Value chart, comparing the bands.

1. The Splash-a-bouts
Rock-n-roll oldies
$2,000 per gig
15 years playing large sized arenas and events

2. The Waves
Polka and traditional Polish music
$300 per gig
10 years playing weddings and small parties

3. Big Dive
Current pop and rhythm and blues
$650 per gig
2 years playing medium-sized arenas and events

> *If we want to solve a problem that we have never solved before, we must leave the door to the unknown ajar.*
>
> —Richard P. Feynman, physicist

CRITERIA	Possible Points	Splash-a-bouts	The Waves	Big Dive
PRICE	10			
EXPERIENCE	10			
MUSIC STYLE	10			
TOTAL POINTS	30			

Literature Connection

Fireman for Life

By Bailey White

I am a first-grade schoolteacher, a small-sized person, not very brave. I have no mechanical sense, loud noises make me jump, and I'm afraid of heights. Why, then, was my hand raised when they called for volunteer firemen down at the community center?

To establish a fire department, we had to have at least eleven volunteers; only ten hands were up. I was in the thrall of that good old rural community spirit. I'll be saving lives and property, I thought, raising my hand higher and higher. It was a noble gesture. Besides, I told myself later that night in a saner moment, surely, in a month or two, someone will come along and take my place.

Our training course lasted ten weeks. Every Tuesday and Thursday night from six to ten o'clock we were down at the agricenter tying slipless knots, scrambling up and down ladders with heavy equipment, and learning about toxic gases, types of fire streams, and the laws of heat flow. We squirted great holes and troughs in the sawdust of the stockyard with a two-and-a-half-inch nozzle, and we spent a lot of time crawling around blindfolded in the livestock arena rescuing each other. I was everyone's favorite victim. I'm easy to drag.

I had nightmares about "flashover"—instant and complete conflagration—and being shut into hot, tight, dark, smoky places. My replacement didn't appear.

It came time to order our "turnout gear." It didn't come in my size. The sleeves of the smallest coat covered my hands. The smallest pants were so big that I tripped over the cuffs as I climbed the ladder. My suit had to be specially made. It took three months. When I pulled it out of the box, it looked like evening garb for one of Beatrix Potter's rats. It fit perfectly.

There were contests to see who could get completely outfitted in under two minutes. I always ended up three minutes late, with several female snaps whose male counterparts could not be found, and the red suspenders between my legs.

"But I don't want to be a fireman," I complained to our chief. "I'm not good at it. I'm a schoolteacher. Can't you find someone to take my place?"

"With what that suit cost the county," said our frugal chief, Lamar, "you're going to be a fireman for life—or until you can talk some little shrimp of a volunteer into taking over your gear." No shrimps showed up. It looked like I was going to be a fireman for a long time.

I started getting used to it. They elected me secretary, because of my neat first-grade teacher printing, and they taught me how to work the pumper. I wait for the man at the end of the line to holler, "Charge it!" Then I flip three switches and make the gauge read 100 pounds before I open the valve. I also scrub the hose after every fire. Not very heroic.

The other day though, I got my chance. There was a wreck on 84, a head-on collision. Our jobs were to disconnect the batteries of both cars, wash any spilled gasoline off the road, direct traffic, and help the emergency medical technicians. I was at my station, ready to "charge it." But there was no spilled gas. Lamar was directing traffic.

A woman was lying in the grass beside the road. She looked dead to me, but the EMTs, who are finer judges of these things, were hovering over her, monitoring her diminishing vital signs and giving her little puffs of oxygen through a tube up her nose. One of the EMTs motioned me over.

"Her Bible. She wants her Bible. See if you can find it," he whispered earnestly.

The road was strewn with debris: broken glass, papers, a rug, a dog leash, a Mickey Mouse hat—but no Bible. I rummaged through the wreckage frantically. I remembered the story of Stonewall Jackson, whose life had been saved when the Bible he carried over his heart deflected a Yankee bullet. Maybe this was life or death!

Finally, peering through a chink into the trunk of the car, I spotted it. The trunk was jammed shut. I got a crowbar from the fire truck and prized it open. But the book wasn't a Bible. Instead, it was a dog-eared, much-read copy of *Lady Chatterley's Lover*.

What was I to do? Should I tell the EMT there's no Bible? But she was so pale and so still. I had read about the enormous power of suggestion. The book had the heft and bulk of a Bible. I could just . . . but what if she died? The God some people believe in would send a person straight to hell if she died with *Lady Chatterley's Lover* in her hands.

Then something came over me. It felt like the same thing that had made me raise my hand in the community center. I took the book and placed it on her chest. I folded her hands on top of it. She hugged it and caressed the cover.

Within minutes the color rose to her cheeks, her eyes fluttered open, she snuffed a long drag of oxygen through the tube, moaned, and said, "Where am I? What's happening to me?" And as she gazed into the relieved face of the EMT, I deftly tweaked the book from her grasp and replaced it in the trunk of the car.

I may not be the biggest, bravest fireman in my county, but on that day, with a little help from D.H. Lawrence, I'm pretty sure I saved a life. It gave me a heady feeling.

Last week Lamar called me up. "There's a little man here. About your size. Wants to be a fireman. Want to let him try on your suit?"

"Nope," I said, "I'm a fireman for life."

The author tells the reader about two important decisions she made—to volunteer for the new fire department and to substitute a novel for the Bible that the injured woman requested.

On what basis did she make each decision? What issues made her decisions difficult?

"Fireman for Life," from *Mama Makes Up Her Mind and Other Dangers of Southern Living* by Bailey White. Copyright ©1993 by Bailey White. Reprinted by permission of Addison-Wesley Publishing Co.

Getting with the Program

For months, Michaela has been asking Amy to take programming classes with her after work. She wants both of them to be more knowledgeable when customers call with computer system problems.

Amy's attitude from the beginning has been that customer support representatives such as Michaela and herself should let the company's programmers figure out what's wrong when a customer calls. As a young mother, she has big responsibilities at home, and doesn't feel she is paid enough to give up personal time to learn something that other people in the company can do for her.

"Amy," Michaela says one morning, "I've registered for the new classes that start next month. If you don't take them now, you may not get another chance until next year."

"Michaela, no way," Amy snaps. "I don't have time, and I don't need to know programming for this job. What I need is more money and less pressure."

Three weeks later, a memo announcing a new division of the company appears on Amy's desk. Customer service representatives with moderate knowledge of computer programming may choose to work with their clients directly from home two days a week.

Amy loves the idea of being able to stay home with her children. She immediately rushes to register for the classes. When she arrives to register, she finds that the classes are full—and eight people are ahead of her on the waiting list.

 With a partner, make a list of problem-solving strategies to help Amy with her predicament. Be prepared to share your ideas with the class.

_____

_____

_____

> " *In any moment of decision, the best thing you can do is the right thing, the next best thing is the wrong thing, and the worse thing you can do is nothing.* "
>
> —Theodore Roosevelt, 26th U.S. President

PRACTICE

1. In our personal lives and our careers, we make decisions on a constant basis. On a separate sheet of paper, list at least one long-range decision, one medium-range decision, and one short-range decision regarding goals in your personal life. Repeat the process concerning goals in your career. In a short paragraph, evaluate those decisions based on the methods discussed in this workshop.

2. Consider a recent decision you made or need to make at work or at home. Construct a T-chart listing the positives and negatives associated with the decision. Be prepared to share your completed chart with a partner.

3. Using the Internet or other resources, find a problem-solving success story that involved a team of people working together with a shared goal. How did a common vision aid the resolution of the problem? Report your findings to the class.

SUMMARY

➤ Considering the timeline or deadline for a particular problem or question is an effective way to categorize and manage decisions.

➤ There are always decisions to be made—it is a lifelong process. Decision-making steps are like spokes in a wheel that never stops turning.

➤ When solving a problem depends on the joint efforts of a team, the first step is to establish common goals.

➤ Simple T-charts and Decision Value charts will help you to solve the most complex problems.

➤ Knowing how to distinguish symptoms from problems is a key part of identifying problems.

➤ When viewed as an opportunity, decision making in the face of change can be an advantage instead of a problem.

1. Discuss the difference between symptoms and problems. Why it is important to identify the problem?

   _____

   _____

2. Discuss the differences between proactive, reactive, and no-action thinkers. Identify organizations or people that fit each category.

   _____

   _____

3. List the three types of decisions and define each.

   _____

   _____

4. What are the decision-making steps? What are some additional components to consider when making a decision?

   _____

   _____

5. Define a T-chart and a Decision Value chart. What are their uses in the decision-making process?

   _____

   _____

6. Find an example of a problem resulting from change in the workplace. Analyze how it can be turned into an advantage.

   _____

   _____

PROJECTS

1. Keep a journal for at least three days listing all the decisions you make in your personal life. Be sure to include any changes that impacted your original decisions. What decision-making and/or problem-solving methods did you use?

2. Write a review of a television or movie drama/mystery identifying the problem-solving and/or decision-making techniques used. Include any additional decision-making components and changes that were important to the final outcome.

3. Using the Internet as at least one of your information sources, create a poster-sized Decision Value chart regarding one of the following decisions:

- Changing jobs
- Purchasing a car, truck, or motorcycle
- Traveling by car, plane, or train

©2001 PhotoDisc, Inc.

When solving a problem depends on the joint efforts of a team, the first step is to establish common goals.

GOALS

⟳ Understand the importance of effective listening in resolving differences.

⟳ Discover effective listening strategies.

⟳ Identify "speaking to share" strategies.

HEAR NO EVIL, SPEAK NO EVIL

"Be a good listener. Your ears will never get you in trouble," author Frank Tyger said. That excellent advice is especially useful during conflict. Negotiations often fail because one or both sides stop listening to the other. Instead, each side focuses on arguing the "rightness" of their positions. This workshop provides vital tools for becoming an effective listener during conflict. Your good listening skills will allow you to genuinely hear the other side *and* sensitively express your position.

Crossed Wires

Maria and Loretta work for the same company. They were once good friends, but never see each other anymore. Loretta misses Maria and wonders why they don't get together. One day, they pass each other in the hall.

Maria: So much has been happening!

Loretta: Oh, really? Like what?

Maria: Mark and I and our new neighbors have been so busy going to movies and cooking out, I seem to have forgotten my other friends! I'm so sorry!

Loretta: Well, if you're having fun, that's great. No need to feel sorry for me.

Maria: Oh, I don't feel sorry for you . . .

Loretta: Good! *(She leaves in a huff.)*

✔ **What listening techniques could have been used to avoid this confusion?**

TOOLS OF THE TRADE

Effective Listening

Your ability to listen well can be your most powerful tool for resolving a dispute. Effective listeners practice the following three guidelines.

1. **Give the other person your full attention.** Avoid interrupting, look directly at the other person, and minimize distractions.

2. **Encourage the other person to talk.** Make good eye contact and nod your head to show that you understand what the other person is saying. Lean forward and use supportive phrases such as "Oh, I see" and "Really?" to help the speaker know you're listening and interested. Relax and focus on what is being said and how it is being said.

3. **Show the other person that you want to understand.** Ask questions to show the other person that you want to understand, not judge. Use neutral language, and restate the speaker's words. For example: "When you say you won't let me use the car because I can't take care of it, I'm not sure I understand. Do you mean you don't think I'll replace the gas I use?"

Speaking to Share

When you listen calmly and effectively, it helps the other person listen to you in the same way. "Speaking to share"—projecting an open, approachable listening style—will set an example of how others should listen to you.

➤ **Refer to what the other person said.** Let the speaker know that you heard what was said, and that what was said made an impact. *"Wow . . . so you were really hurt by what she said."*

➤ **Look for signs of understanding.** If the other person does not appear to be listening or understanding, ask questions or restate your point. *"Let me put it a different way; I think that swapping shifts can benefit everyone."*

➤ **Take a chance and open up.** Tell the other person how important it is to you to be understood. When you say what you believe, explain why you believe it. *"It's really important that you understand where I'm coming from on this. Allowing us to swap shifts benefits everyone, and the company."*

Key Ideas

★ **listening**—making a conscious effort to hear; paying close attention to what others are saying

★ **understanding**—knowing or grasping what is meant; interpreting; having a thorough comprehension of a subject

★ **speaking to share**—projecting an open, approachable listening style

> *When you talk, you repeat what you already know; when you listen, you often learn something.*
>
> —Jared Sparks,
> Unitarian minister and historian

Defusing the Emotional Bomb

Part of the listening process is learning to deal with your emotions. Feelings about other people and about problems can have a strong affect on conflict resolution. Those feelings you may have about the person or the problem, however, are not as important as the way you handle those feelings. Some strategies for handling emotions during conflict follow.

➤ **Count and breathe.** This age-old technique is very effective. Take a deep breath, and start to count. If counting to 10 doesn't help, try taking two breaths and counting to 20. Feel the tension in your chest flow out as you exhale.

➤ **Take a brisk walk.** Exercise will burn off the excess adrenaline that fuels your feelings of anxiety and stress. Exercise releases endorphins, potent groups of natural chemicals in the body that may block anxiety and help you cope with stressful situations.

➤ **In a crisis, think challenge.** Think of opportunities—not obstacles—when you approach stressful situations. A positive outlook will give you a boost of energy.

➤ **You can't disagree with an emotion.** When people feel angry with you, telling them they shouldn't be angry will only increase the anger. Instead, you should acknowledge their emotions and calmly share your own.

➤ **Watch your self-talk.** Self-talk is what you say to yourself throughout the day, during a confrontation, or any time you think before you act. What you say to yourself can affect your emotions, self-confidence, and effectiveness as a problem solver.

➤ **Find the cause.** Once you identify the emotion, try to understand what is causing it. Sometimes people act angry with others when they are actually disappointed with themselves. Trying to blame yourself or others almost always gets in the way of solving a problem or improving a relationship.

> *Listen—or thy tongue will keep thee deaf.*
>
> —Native-American Proverb

Make good eye contact and nod your head to show that you under-stand what the other person is saying.

©2001 PhotoDisc, Inc.

THE STANDOFF
Segment 2

Meet David and Julian. David sells computerized communication systems; Julian installs them. This video demonstrates how their differing needs and constraints lead to conflict. Follow the conflict as told by both parties, from its inception to its win-win resolution. As you watch the conflict between David and Julian, analyze their use of effective listening.

Before David and Julian can resolve the problem, they must understand what the other is up against.

Post-Viewing Questions

1. How did David and Julian use good communication skills to negotiate a solution to their problem?

_____

_____

_____

2. When was listening essential for a win-win outcome?

_____

_____

_____

In One Ear and Out the Other

At 8:15 a.m. in the hotel restaurant, half a dozen people who have finished breakfast are lining up to pay their bills. Most of them want to add the charge to their hotel tabs, but Jack, the new employee at the computerized cash register, is struggling with the system. It seems that, to assign a charge to a room, he has to go through three different computer screens, and this morning the hotel's network is running at turtle speed.

The people in line are fidgeting and muttering to each other. Jack would rather toss the bills in a pile and deal with them later, but Rosalee, the manager, specifically told him not to do that. As Jack finishes with one customer and begins the long process over again with the next, a waiter named Hank glides up beside him.

"Didn't Rosalee explain how to handle charges to the rooms?" Hank says in a low voice. "There's a much quicker way. Here, I'll show you." Gently nudging Jack away from the keyboard, Hank hits a combination of keys. The room charge screen pops up in two seconds. "See?" he murmurs to Jack. In a moment, Hank completes the transaction, and the grateful customer is out the door.

Hank explains the procedure once more, naming the keys as he points to them. "Okay, that will help you, won't it?" Hank asks. "Let me know if you have any more problems."

"Yeah, right," Jack grumbles, embarrassed about receiving instructions from a waiter in front of all the restaurant patrons. After all, he's a manager in training! Jack tries to apply Hank's shortcut for the next patron, but realizes he can't. He was so angry and upset—he didn't listen to anything Hank had told him.

> **"I listen from within."**
>
> —Thomas Edison

Research has shown that negative reactions to advice are generally stronger if the advice giver is "similar" to the recipient (i.e., in terms of age, status, or gender). Do you think Jack would have been more receptive if Rosalee, instead of Hank, had shown him the shortcut?

_____

_____

_____

_____

PRACTICE

1. Can you think of other ways to listen effectively, or more ways to help other people listen to you? Brainstorm in groups, and create a list to share with the class.

2. As an entire class, play the childhood game "Telephone." One person whispers a message to the person next to her, who in turn whispers it to the person next to him, and so it goes until everyone has heard the message. The last person states the message out loud, and the first person evaluates how close it is to the original message. Discuss with the class how the lack of effective listening skills impacted the message.

3. Enter an educational chatroom or Web board on the Internet. "Chat" for about 10 minutes. Write about how Internet speaking and listening differ from face-to-face interactions. What happens to emotions in each venue? What are the benefits and the disadvantages of each? Be prepared to share your findings with the rest of the class.

SUMMARY

➤ Your ability to listen well can be your most powerful tool for resolving a dispute.

➤ "Speaking to share"—projecting an open, approachable listening style—will set an example of how others should listen to you.

➤ Part of the listening process is learning to deal with your emotions.

Your good listening skills will allow you to genuinely hear the other side and sensitively express your position.

Nelson Mandela: The Peaceful Negotiator

One of the 20th century's great world leaders, Nelson Mandela was born in a tribal village in South Africa in 1918. He spent his boyhood herding cattle and was destined to become a chief of his people, but he left home to attend school and become a lawyer.

Mandela dedicated himself early in life to ending the long-standing policies of racial segregation set forth by a white-dominated government. Through his law practice, Mandela worked tirelessly for social and economic equality in South Africa. In the 1940s, he became a leader of the African National Congress (ANC), a black-liberation group. As a young man, he advocated non-violent methods to end the social and economic divides between blacks and whites in South Africa. But increasing violence towards unarmed black civilians and the outlawing of the ANC ultimately led Mandela to accept a more militant approach and engage in acts of sabotage against the South African regime.

©Corbis/Paul Velasco

In 1962, Mandela was put on trial for treason and later sentenced to life imprisonment. For 27 years, he remained a political prisoner and during that time underwent many personal changes. While in prison, Mandela read widely, wrote many insightful letters, and used the time to meditate and reflect on his lifelong struggle for freedom. He earned the respect not only of his fellow inmates, but also of his captors and the outside world.

With wide support among South Africa's black population and the international community, Mandela eventually negotiated his release in 1990, and, in a remarkable gesture, forgave his oppressors. Instead of expressing feelings of bitterness and vengeance, Mandela showed a compassion and understanding that would eventually change the face of South Africa and earn him the admiration of people around the globe.

After long, peaceful negotiations, Nelson Mandela succeeded in putting an end to the legacy of racial segregation and social injustice in his country. In 1993, he was awarded the prestigious Nobel Peace Prize, and in 1994, the entire world watched as South Africa held its first democratic, all-race elections. Fittingly, it was Nelson Mandela who was voted in as president, an office he held until his retirement in 1999. Mandela's lifelong dream of a free and democratic society for all South Africans had finally come true.

REVIEW QUESTIONS

1. Define listening and understanding.

   _____

   _____

2. What strategies does an effective listener use?

   _____

   _____

3. What are three behaviors of people who speak to share?

   _____

   _____

4. What are three strategies for defusing emotions during a conflict?

   _____

   _____

PROJECTS

1. Effective listening is a crucial component of many professions. Make an appointment with a school counselor or social worker to collect some more tips on becoming a good listener. Take along the lists of skills presented in this workshop, and share it with the person you interview. Ask for other suggestions to add to the list. If there is time, ask the person to describe his or her most difficult or most interesting listening experience, and to tell you how he or she became a good listener. Take notes, and share what you learn with the class.

2. Watch a television interview. Keeping in mind the listening skills you learned in this workshop, watch for indications that the interviewer and interviewee are listening to each other. Make a note of any misunderstandings that occur, and write a summary of your observations. Share your findings with the class.

GOALS

- Understand how advice and criticism can lead to conflict.
- Identify strategies for giving and receiving advice and criticism.
- Discover methods for controlling anger and stress.

©2001 PhotoDisc, Inc.

ACCEPT WITH THANKS

A coworker criticizes you during a department meeting. You offer a good idea, but your supervisor dismisses it as "irrelevant." Someone you supervise accuses you of playing favorites. How would you react to these scenarios? Would you stay calm? Would you be upset? How we accept—and give—criticism and guidance is crucial to conflict prevention. This workshop offers successful methods for defusing anger and misunderstandings when giving and receiving criticism and advice.

Strictly Business

When Chad got to work this morning, he overheard Kathy talking to Joan. "Finally, he's here! Wouldn't you like to keep his hours, late every day?" hissed Kathy. "He doesn't even try to get here on time," Joan retorted.

Chad didn't know what to say. He had to take his children to the babysitter's in the morning, and had his supervisor's approval to come in late and stay late, to make up the time. Chad didn't believe in sharing his personal life with his business associates. He did his job—they had nothing to complain about.

"Well, should we start work on the Miller project?" he asked them, ignoring their remarks. "Oh, if you're finally ready, we are too!" Kathy replied rudely.

✔ ***What can Chad do to maintain his privacy and improve his work relations?***

TOOLS OF THE TRADE

Responding to Criticism

When people are criticized, defenses immediately surface. Often, a first response is to shut the other person out—to stop listening. When we refuse to be open to criticism, we potentially miss good information, the opportunity to benefit from it, and future advice from that person. Even worse, we increase our chances of misinterpreting the other person's attitudes and motives, and increase the potential for conflict. The following four steps will improve your ability to respond to criticism.

> **Put aside your ego.** Separate your pride from the criticism as much as you possibly can. If you receive criticism about a particular task, remind yourself that only that task is in question, not your overall performance—and certainly not your worth as a human being.

> **Suspend judgment.** Don't decide immediately whether the other person is right or wrong or jump to conclusions about their motivations or attitudes.

> **Listen hard to the advice itself.** Get beyond emotions and tone of voice, and concentrate fully on the message itself.

> **Use active listening techniques.** Take an active role in the conversation to make sure you've understood the advice or criticism. Paraphrase what the speaker has said and ask if your version is correct. Ask further questions to clarify any points.

Key Ideas

★ **advice**—counsel or suggestion as to a course of action

★ **criticism**—severe judgment or censure

★ **active listening**—the act of playing an active role in the listening process, which includes questioning and clarifying information

Encouraging Feedback

Once you begin encouraging helpful comments rather than reacting defensively, you may find that something amazing occurs—your relationships with others dramatically improve. Lending an attentive ear to advice makes others feel useful and appreciated. To encourage polite feedback from others, practice the following tips.

> Be approachable. Let others know you will listen to advice.

> Convey your attentiveness with eye contact.

> Use positive body language. Keep your posture relaxed—don't cross your arms or fidget.

> Don't make excuses or blame others; those reactions sound defensive.

> Thank the person for his or her help.

> If appropriate, ask for further suggestions.

> If you do adopt someone's advice, tell that person you have done so. Even if you don't follow the suggestions, let the person know that you considered them seriously.

Constructive Advice and Criticism

As important as it is to be able to receive advice and criticism openly, it is equally important to be able to offer advice and constructive criticism effectively. Remember, the term "constructive" means to build, so make sure the advice you offer will benefit the receiver.

Constructive advice and criticism is:

> ➤ **Nonjudgmental and issue-focused.** Constructive advice doesn't convey judgment of the other person. It concentrates on the difficulty at hand, not on the qualities of the person you're advising.

> ➤ **Balanced and mutual.** Constructive advice frames the issue as a mutual problem to be solved, not as a problem that the other person must solve alone. Constructive advice balances the positive and negative. Always state the positive before you get to the negative, and reinforce the positive at the end of the conversation.

> ➤ **Focused on the present.** Constructive advice deals with today's problems; it doesn't dredge up matters from the past.

> ➤ **Empathetic.** Constructive advice shows that you care about how the other person is feeling. When giving constructive advice or criticism, the speaker conveys the sense that the listener may have a different—and valid—perspective on the situation.

> ➤ **Focused on "I," not "you."** To avoid directly accusing the other person, make it clear that the reactions you're stating are your own. Use first-person singular pronouns such as "I," "me," and "myself." This strategy allows the listener to appreciate your motivation, improves mutual understanding, and increases the chance that the listener will take your comments to heart.

> ➤ **Accurate, specific, and timely.** Before you criticize or advise someone, make sure you have the facts exactly right. Deliver your information clearly, and be specific. Don't wait too long to address a problem. Choose a time when the person is calm, not too busy to listen to you, and free of distraction. To avoid interruptions and potential embarrassment, pick a quiet place.

Stress Blockers

The basic stress reducers will also help you manage your anger.

> ➤ Take some deep breaths.
> ➤ Visualize a relaxing experience.
> ➤ Exercise until you're tired and ready to relax.
> ➤ Take a warm bath or a long shower.
> ➤ Listen to a soothing CD or tape.

Seven Steps for Managing Anger

No matter how much we are provoked, anger is never our first response. In fact, it is what psychologists call a "secondary" emotion. Anger stems from a "primary" emotion, such as embarrassment, shame, disappointment, frustration, fear, or resentment. Anger is a response that helps you cope with being vulnerable, but it can have serious external and internal consequences when not managed appropriately. Follow the tips below to keep your anger in check.

➤ **Accept the fact that you're angry.** Acknowledge your responsibility for dealing with the emotion.

➤ **Decide exactly what you're angry about.** Analyze the source of your feelings, and separate the real problem from insignificant matters. Identify deep emotions underlying the surface problem.

➤ **Be sure you understand the facts of the situation.** Confirm the facts; don't waste energy being angry about a misunderstanding.

➤ **Find someone to speak to about the problem.** Usually the best person to address is the one at whom you're angry. If that is not possible, choose a neutral party whom you trust to give good advice.

➤ **When you speak up, do it in an assertive—not aggressive—manner.** Use constructive advice skills. Describe the problem objectively, describe your feelings, describe your needs and desires, and focus on the goal you want to achieve.

➤ **Propose a solution.** Find a resolution that is acceptable to you and potentially acceptable to the other person.

➤ **Reflect on the experience and learn from it.** Think about whether you managed your anger in the best possible way. Then decide whether you should modify your approach in the future.

> *When angry, count to ten before you speak; if very angry, count to a hundred.*
>
> —Thomas Jefferson, 3rd U.S. President

Ethics & Etiquette

Many companies have a conflict of interest policy, which typically requires employees to avoid any business transactions that place personal interest or personal gain over that of the company. For example, employees might be offered gifts or invitations to entertainment events from a supplier. A conflict of interest can also occur when an employee or family member has a direct or indirect personal or financial interest in a company's supplier, partner, competitor, or customer. What other examples can you think of that would constitute a conflict of interest?

DISHING IT OUT

Did you know that managers often say they give constructive criticism, but subordinates just as often say they don't receive any criticism that's constructive? How can both statements be true? Often, when people *think* they are giving constructive advice or criticism, the words and tone they choose imply the opposite. You have already discovered the importance of becoming a good listener. Equally as important is your ability to effectively convey advice and criticism. Though this is true in all interactions with others, it is especially important when you're the boss.

> *Our success—in the workplace and in life—is directly correlated with our ability to hear criticism. That is how we learn.*
>
> —Hendrie Weisinger, psychologist

The following comments from supervisors may have some grain of truth in them, but the way the information is presented will make the receiver feel hurt and annoyed. This kind of criticism leads to defensive behaviors and will not result in positive outcomes. Using what you've learned about constructive advice, rewrite each statement. Make sure to convert each comment to an "I" statement.

©2001 PhotoDisc, Inc.

1. "You're always late. Why can't you get to work on time?"

2. "If you weren't always so hyper, you'd see we can't rush this job. There's too much at stake."

3. "That's just a silly idea. It's not going to work."

On the Net

For more detailed information about the field of conflict resolution, including links to hundreds of articles, organizations, and Web resources, check out these great sites:

www.crinfo.org

http://isca.indiana.edu/conflict.html

War at the Drugstore

Jana has worked in a busy drugstore for almost five years. The owner, who is pleased with Jana's work, let her know that she is in line to become assistant manager. Jana is dedicated and smart. That's why it pains her to see the new pharmacist, Raisa, making such a muddle of things.

Jana thinks Raisa has no sense of how to prioritize her work. This morning, when Raisa arrived 12 minutes late, there was a stack of prescription slips waiting to be filled. Customers brought in some; doctors phoned in others. Did Raisa check to see which were most urgent? No. Looking nervous about the amount of work she had to do, she started filling prescriptions in a seemingly random order.

> **"** *He has the right to criticize who has the heart to help.* **"**
>
> —Abraham Lincoln, 16th U.S. President

Jana notices a long-time customer, Mr. Gretzky, standing with his cane, looking wobbly and dismayed. At this point, Jana feels she has to intervene.

Jana: Do you have a script for Gretzky?

Raisa: Who?

Jana: Mr. Gretzky—he's over there waiting. It's probably for his heart pills. You know, it's hard for him to stand around a long time, so you should work on his prescription right away.

Raisa: *(quickly)* Oh, nobody told me.

Jana: You can see him standing there. And all the scripts are marked—pickup, delivery, or in-store customer. You know, if you'd get here on time, you wouldn't fall behind.

Raisa: *(Raisa glares as she yanks a slip from the pile.)* There! Gretzky—it's for an antifungal agent, not heart medicine. You know, I *am* a licensed pharmacist!

Jana: *(snaps)* Well, if Mr. Gretzky has a heart attack in the store, it will be your fault!

Storming off, Jana thinks, "I'm just trying to help people, and see what I get for it!"

 With a partner, rewrite this interaction using effective listening, constructive criticism, and anger management skills. Be prepared to role-play your edited script for the class.

1. Assume you are beginning a team project in which Robert, notorious for being uncooperative and ill tempered, has to play a major role. Think about how you might approach Robert to advise him to cooperate during the project. How could you begin? What points could you make? Write some of the things you might say to Robert. Be prepared to share your results with the class.

2. Think of a situation when you were severely angry. Describe how you could have handled it better, using the "Seven Steps for Managing Anger." Begin by describing the situation. Then, write what you could have done for each of the seven steps.

3. For each of the following situations, examine the "you" message and convert it to an "I" message.

a. You are working on an important project. A coworker keeps interrupting. "You shouldn't ever interrupt someone when you see he is busy."

b. Jane doesn't answer letters promptly. "You're hired to get those letters out. Do it. Don't procrastinate."

c. Your boss doesn't tell you things you need to know. "You never tell me anything. How do you expect me to know what's going on?"

4. Discover more ideas for improving your listening skills. Explore the Web site of the International Listening Association, at http://www.listen.org. Check out the listening exercises and the quotes about listening. Take notes about the new skills you uncover and share them with the class.

SUMMARY

➤ How we accept—and give—criticism and advice is crucial to conflict prevention.

➤ Lending an attentive ear to advice makes others feel useful and appreciated.

➤ Remember, the term "constructive" means to build, so make sure the advice you offer will benefit the receiver.

➤ Anger is a response that helps you cope with being vulnerable, but it can have serious external and internal consequences when not managed appropriately.

REVIEW QUESTIONS

1. List the four steps for improving your ability to respond to criticism.

   _____

2. Why is encouraging feedback important to effective relationships?

   _____

3. What is constructive criticism or advice?

   _____

4. List the seven steps for effectively managing anger. Explain the significance of each step.

   _____

PROJECTS

1. Imagine you work for a company that provides computer support services. You and a fellow technician upgraded the network in a major client's office, installing new hardware and software. In your opinion, your coworker tends to be a little sloppy, but you personally checked the entire system before you left, and it worked perfectly. The client seemed happy at the time. This morning, the department secretary tells you that the client complained to your supervisor about the network's performance. You know the boss is upset; though nothing has been said. With a partner, write a role-play showing how to handle this situation.

2. Keep a journal for a week, documenting situations where you became angry and the techniques you used to manage that anger. What was the result of your anger in each situation?

3. In a one-week time span, list the number of times you hear people using "I" statements. Also list the situations in which the "I" statements occurred, and what affect you felt they had on the situation.

4. Offer constructive criticism to a coworker, friend, or family member at least three times (different person each time). Remember to utilize the skills learned in this workshop. Write a summary of your experience. What was your criticism? How was it presented, and how was it received? Record how you felt during the experience.

GOALS

➡ Discover the importance of negotiation in problem solving.

➡ Distinguish between formal and informal negotiating.

➡ Learn interpersonal skills and steps of effective negotiation.

©2001 PhotoDisc, Inc.

AT THE BARGAINING TABLE

In spring of 1997, 185,000 members of the Teamsters' union walked out on their jobs at UPS. Negotiations about drivers' wages and full-time benefits had been going on for four months with no resolutions. The strike, which lasted only 15 days, cost UPS $300 million per week in lost revenues and the Teamsters' union $10 million per week in strike benefits paid to its members. Whether the potential losses for both sides are large or small, the ability to reach a sensible agreement depends upon each party's ability to negotiate. This workshop illustrates the value of effective negotiating skills, and provides methods for making positive, constructive agreements when you're at the bargaining table.

Let's Make a Deal

Carlton has a big date tonight. He bought a new shirt and made reservations, but realized that he forgot one very important thing when he saw his younger sister washing the car.

"Hey, what's going on, Tina? I'm using the car tonight," Carlton said.

"No way, big brother. I need it for the concert," Tina replied.

Carlton told Tina he would pay her $30 if she would let him use the car. Tina agreed. Carlton was out $30, and Tina took a bus to the concert.

 Do you think Carlton and Tina's agreement was fair?

TOOLS OF THE TRADE

Formal and Informal Negotiations

Not all negotiations are equal. Sometimes, a negotiation is a simple matter of a husband and wife deciding what kind of car to buy. Negotiations can also be serious and complex, such as a trade agreement between quarreling countries. Generally, negotiations fall into two main categories—formal and informal.

> **Formal negotiations.** Though they vary according to seriousness, formal negotiations always involve a signed contract. Examples of formal negotiations include resolving a labor dispute or settling a legal action outside of court.

> **Informal negotiations.** Much more casual than formal negotiations, informal negotiations do not necessarily require signed contracts. Verbal agreements between family, coworkers, and friends are the most common type of informal negotiations.

Negotiation Roles

When a negotiation team is formed, roles are not usually assigned—they tend to form naturally as a result of the personalities of group members.

> **Lead negotiator**—speaks for the group
> **Gatekeeper**—limits the time allowed to long-winded talkers and encourages quiet members to share their views
> **Regulator**—helps the group stay on task
> **Tension reliever**—uses humor to ease uncomfortable situations
> **Harmonizer**—mediates differing viewpoints
> **Supporter**—agrees with the ideas of others

Functional and Dysfunctional Negotiation Behaviors

Members of negotiating teams exhibit behaviors that can be described as either functional or dysfunctional. Functional behaviors help the team reach its goals, while dysfunctional behaviors obstruct the team's goals.

FUNCTIONAL BEHAVIORS	DYSFUNCTIONAL BEHAVIORS
Setting goals	Distracting
Seeking information	Dominating
Elaborating ideas	Always opposing
Summarizing	Making irrelevant comments

Key Ideas

★ **negotiation**—the process of attempting to resolve differences in order to reach agreements

★ **arbitration**—the process of settling a dispute between two or more parties by an unbiased third party

★ **binding arbitration**—an arbitration decision of a neutral third party that all parties in a dispute agree to accept

★ **mediator**—an impartial person or team that comes in when two quarreling parties formally agree to have a third party help to resolve the conflict

37

Steps for Successful Negotiating

Sometimes, when formal negotiations continue for a long time with no resolution in sight, both sides agree to arbitration. In such cases, a third party examines both positions and offers a solution. If the parties agree to "binding" arbitration, they must accept the arbitrator's decision, whether they like it or not. Generally, however, negotiators would rather settle disputes themselves. To avoid negotiating "deadlocks," practice the bargaining techniques below.

1. Be prepared.
2. Listen actively.
3. Ask questions.
4. Be willing to give and take.
5. Respect the other negotiator's position.
6. Offer creative solutions and/or closure.

🚫 Not Quite

As assistant general manager for Moby Construction Corp., part of Sam's job includes negotiating with clients who plan to build new homes. Recently, Sam has been losing bids for potential projects. In one negotiation, a young couple who had little experience dealing with the construction industry grew upset with Sam when he failed to discuss various options with them. Sam didn't realize the couple had met with three competing firms and learned about the range of possibilities available to them. Instead of providing alternatives to the couple, Sam gave ultimatums, coming across as a stubborn and pushy negotiator.

Sam also neglected to find any common points of interest. For example, rather than listen to the couple's needs and questions, Sam structured his presentation by expressing his own ideas and plans. As a result, Sam's aggressiveness and insensitivity turned the couple away.

✓ Got It Right

As a sales representative for Sound Alarm Systems Inc., Sally meets daily with potential clients who want to install new alarm systems in their homes and businesses. The alarm business is highly competitive. As a rule, during negotiations, Sally provides potential clients with all the viable options her company offers. She begins by listening to her customers' needs and cost range. Sally also knows that silence can be a powerful tool in negotiating, and gives clients time to absorb and think about her offers and suggestions.

Sally never counters an objection or reaction with a negative response, and she rarely says "No." She has brainstormed a list of positive responses, alternatives, and examples to counteract the negatives. By being prepared, open-minded, and willing to listen, Sally has become an excellent negotiator.

VALERIE BARNETT, FEDERAL MEDIATOR: NEGOTIATING A SOLUTION

Segment 3

Meet Valerie Barnett, a mediator with the Federal Mediation and Conciliation Service. This government agency helps businesses and workers to settle strikes and other employer-employee conflicts. Valerie will explain various elements of the negotiating process, including the importance of communication skills, body language, listening, and understanding. As you watch examples of workplace conflict, think about what it means to reach an agreement based on fairness.

An expert at negotiation and mediation, Valerie Barnett understands the significance of effective verbal and nonverbal communication.

Post-Viewing Questions

1. What is the difference between formal and informal negotiation?

_____

_____

2. What is the role of a mediator?

_____

_____

3. What is "reaching an agreement based on fairness"?

_____

_____

Literature Connection

Eureka College Commencement Address

Given by President Ronald Reagan

May 9, 1982

The following excerpt is a portion of a major foreign policy address that Ronald Reagan delivered on the Eureka College campus on the 50th anniversary of his own graduation. Known as the "Eureka Speech," it challenged the Soviet Union to a new era of negotiations to reduce nuclear arms. Designated S.T.A.R.T. (Strategic Arms Reduction Treaty), the speech is heralded as the beginning of the end of the cold war.

During the 1970s, some of us forgot the warning of President Kennedy, who said that the Soviets "have offered to trade us an apple for an orchard. We don't do that in this country." But we came perilously close to doing just that. If East-West relations in the detente era in Europe have yielded disappointment, detente outside of Europe has yielded a severe disillusionment for those who expected a moderation of Soviet behavior. The Soviet Union continues to support Vietnam in its occupation of Kampuchea and its massive military presence in Laos. It is engaged in a war of aggression against Afghanistan. Soviet proxy forces have brought instability and conflict to Africa and Central America.

We are now approaching an extremely important phase in East-West relations as the current Soviet leadership is succeeded by a new generation. Both the current and the new Soviet leadership should realize aggressive policies will meet a firm Western response. On the other hand, a Soviet leadership devoted to improving its people's lives, rather than expanding its armed conquests, will find a sympathetic partner in the West. The West will respond with expanded trade and other forms of cooperation. But all of this depends on Soviet actions. Standing in the Athenian marketplace 2,000 years ago, Demosthenes said, "What sane man would let another man's words rather than his deeds proclaim who is at peace and who is at war with him?"

Peace is not the absence of conflict, but the ability to cope with conflict by peaceful means. I believe we can cope. I believe that the West can fashion a realistic, durable policy that will protect our interests and keep the peace, not just for this generation but for your children and your grandchildren.

How does President Reagan define peace?

What conflict resolution and negotiation strategies did President Reagan use in his speech?

Excerpt from Commencement Address, Eureka College, Illinois, May 9, 1982, by President Ronald Reagan. The Ronald Reagan Presidential Foundation and Ronald Reagan Presidential Library.

Big Deal

In one factory, charges of harassment (nicknames, slurs, negative stereotyping, and hostile pranks) led to a labor dispute. Two experienced machinists allegedly harassed a supervisor to such an extent that the supervisor had them fired for insubordination (disobedience to authority). The machinists' union filed a grievance (a complaint), demanding that the company reinstate the fired workers. When the dispute could not be settled, it was brought before negotiating teams.

The negotiators on both sides came prepared. They carried thick notebooks filled with information, such as employment records of the machinists, transcripts of previous discussions between management and the machinists—even statements from other workers in the plant. Both sides examined and evaluated these pieces of evidence.

In discussions, each side listened carefully to the other. Negotiators observed body language and gestures in order to interpret unspoken meanings. They elaborated and clarified points of confusion, asked follow-up questions, completed their arguments with detailed summaries, and answered questions thoroughly.

> *Let us never negotiate out of fear, but let us never fear to negotiate.*
>
> —John F. Kennedy, 35th U.S. President

 In groups of at least three, role-play this negotiation process. Both sides, and a mediator, should be represented. Upon completion of the role-play, report the result of your negotiation to the group.

DID YOU KNOW?

The "Rule of Three" and Win-Win Negotiations

In negotiations, the "Rule of Three" is the maximum you are willing to ask for or give, the minimum you are willing to accept or pay, and your realistic goal, which is somewhere in the middle. Negotiators should be open to negotiating within that range.

Ideally, negotiations are entered into with a win-win attitude rather than a confrontational attitude. Win-win negotiations are characterized by the belief that both parties can come away from the process with satisfactory results. Both parties respect the other's position, and both choose to cooperate in order to reach an agreement.

PRACTICE

1. Imagine that you and 10 other members of your class are teachers negotiating for a new contract with the school board. Divide the class into groups and role-play the negotiation process. Remember to include the various roles and behaviors used in successful negotiation.

2. With a partner, participate in an informal negotiation process as the two of you decide what kind of car to purchase. Note the skills and methods from this workshop that help you come to agreement.

3. In small groups, use the Internet, the library, or CD-ROM resources to get more information about what it takes to be a skillful negotiator or arbitrator. Present your findings to the class. Visit the American Arbitration Association's Web site at www.adr.org to get started.

SUMMARY

➤ Generally, negotiations fall into two main categories—formal and informal.

➤ When a negotiation team is formed, roles are not usually assigned—they tend to form naturally as a result of the personalities of group members.

➤ Functional behaviors help the team reach its goals, while dysfunctional behaviors obstruct the team's goals.

➤ Sometimes, when negotiations continue for a long time with no resolution in sight, both sides agree to arbitration.

On the Net

Founded in 1919, the International Chamber of Commerce (ICC) is the world's leading organization in the field of international commercial dispute resolution. The ICC's Court of Arbitration works to resolve business disputes between parties of different nationalities, with different linguistic, legal, and cultural backgrounds. To learn more about the ICC, go to:

www.iccwbo.org

REVIEW QUESTIONS

1. Explain the difference between formal negotiations and informal negotiations.

_____

_____

2. How is arbitration different from the ordinary negotiating process?

_____

_____

3. Summarize a negotiation you participated in recently. Describe any steps to successful negotiating that were used.

_____

_____

PROJECTS

1. Interview the manager of a large company in your community. Ask about negotiations in which he or she has participated, and record his or her perceptions about why the negotiations were successful or unsuccessful. Create a chart outlining your findings, and prepare a report that explains the situation.

2. With a small group, use the library, the Internet, or CD-ROM resources to find out about labor disputes that were settled through binding arbitration. Prepare a report about the settlements. Include quotes from the parties involved, and further elaborate your findings with charts.

> *The problems that exist in the world today cannot be solved by the level of thinking that created them.*
>
> —Albert Einstein

GOALS

➭ Understand the role of "fairness" in arriving at a solution.

➭ Brainstorm to invent creative solutions that benefit both sides of a conflict.

©2001 PhotoDisc, Inc.

FAIR AND SQUARE

"It is not fair to ask of others what you are not willing to do yourself," Eleanor Roosevelt said. Often, in the negotiation process, agreements are made based on who can "hold out" or maintain their argument the longest—not on what works best for all involved. When negotiating an agreement, however, it is essential to think of solutions that would be acceptable to you if you were on the other side of the bargaining table. This workshop focuses on the role of fairness in negotiations and demonstrates brainstorming techniques for finding fair agreements.

Even Steven

Steven is assigning a workspace designed for only four people to his six marketing employees.

Steven gives a diagram to Aaron, Ben, and Carol and asks them to divide the spaces fairly. Not wanting to pass up a golden opportunity, they give themselves slightly more space than the others. "We've been here the longest," Aaron says. "It's only fair."

To the veteran employees' surprise, Steven gives the diagram to Dee, Erykah, and Flora the next day. "I've instructed your coworkers to divide these spaces evenly," Steven says. "Now, you choose where you'd like to sit."

✔ **Do you think Steven's method was fair? Can you think of other solutions?**

TOOLS OF THE TRADE

• •

Common Conflict Solutions

Generally, when we think about solutions to conflicts, we consider the two most common approaches: "either-or" solutions and "splitting it down the middle" solutions.

➤ **Either-or.** When assessing a problem, it is often difficult to see more than two possible solutions: *either* we get what we want and the other side walks away empty-handed, *or* the other side gets what they want and we get nothing.

➤ **Splitting it down the middle.** Another commonly used tactic for solving a problem is "splitting it down the middle." For example, two parties might divide the difference between a $100 asking price and a $50 offer and come up with a $75 sale.

• •

Creative Negotiating

The main problem with using the "either-or" and "split it down the middle" approaches is that, right from the start, you limit your options for resolving the problem. How do you come up with other possible options for solving a conflict?

➤ **Think of solutions that are based on underlying interests—not positions.** Both "either-or" and "splitting it down the middle" solutions are based on positions, not on underlying interests. When both sides forget their positions and think about what they truly want, creative solutions result.

➤ **Use brainstorming to consider all options.** When you determine the underlying interests, you're ready to brainstorm your way to creative solutions. Brainstorming, which usually involves at least two people, is a strategy for setting our imaginations free to think of all possible resolutions, no matter how foolish they might seem at the time.

Key Ideas

★ **interest**—a true want or attraction

★ **underlying interests**—issues or situations that drive bargaining positions

★ **position**—a policy, view, or opinion, especially an official one

★ **brain-storming**—the unrestrained suggestion of ideas on a topic

★ **fair**—just; honest

★ **standard**—something established for use as a rule or basis of comparison in measuring or judging fairness

Ethics & Etiquette

While negotiating with a customer about a product, you realize she cannot afford your price. After a long and friendly conversation, she thanks you and says she'll have to try another store. You know a competitor who has the same product in her price range. Do you let the customer know? Why or why not?

Rules for Brainstorming in Negotiation

Though brainstorming is essentially a freethinking activity, following the guidelines below will produce the best results.

➤ State the underlying interests of the people involved in the conflict. Then, come up with possible solutions that will satisfy these interests.

➤ Make every possible solution welcome, no matter how crazy it might sound. Don't criticize any ideas during the brainstorming session.

➤ Produce as many ideas as possible.

➤ Play "piggyback." If a good idea is offered, build on top of it.

➤ Write down all of the suggested ideas.

➤ After brainstorming, identify the useful ideas, and discuss them.

What Is Fair?

Determining whether or not a solution is fair can be very difficult, for what is fair often depends on circumstances and opinions. For example, what might be fair between friends could seem unfair between strangers. There are, however, some steps to follow to ensure your solutions are as fair as possible for both sides.

1. **Ask for what is fair.** When you are ready to discuss solutions, avoid stating your proposal as if it were a position. Simply state that you are looking for a solution that is fair.

2. **Establish your standards of fairness.** What facts and elements determine whether something is fair to you? Make sure the other side knows how you decide that something is fair or unfair.

3. **Be open to the other side's standards.** The other side may have different standards of fairness. Listen to their standards with an open mind, and don't be afraid to change your mind about what is fair.

On the Net

To learn more about the benefits, history, and principles of brainstorming and other problem-solving techniques, check out:

www.brainstorming.co.uk

PUT YOUR HEADS TOGETHER

Think about times when you tried to reach formal or informal agreements with others. Did you experience "either-or" thinking? Did you attempt to "split it down the middle"? Did you brainstorm? Think about which strategies produced the best results.

✓ Imagine that you've been working as a product developer for a toy company for over five years. Your supervisor's cousin has just been hired in your department. You've discovered that he has essentially the same job title and responsibilities that you do, but that he is making more money than you—and you've been asked to train him! Before you confront your supervisor, you must brainstorm several resolutions to the problem.

1. Write the problem on a sheet of paper.

2. Set a watch or a timer for three minutes.

3. For three minutes, write down any possible solutions you can think of. Whatever you do, don't stop writing.

4. Don't forget to focus on interests instead of positions.

5. When three minutes are up, stop and review the possible solutions. Share the solutions as a class, writing them on the board.

©2001 PhotoDisc, Inc.

Make every possible solution welcome, no matter how crazy it might sound. Don't criticize any ideas during the brainstorming session.

The Grass Is Greener

While working part-time for a landscaping service that went out of business, Osami learned valuable skills in addition to meeting a number of interesting customers. One of them, Mr. Kincaid, was so pleased with Osami's work that he asked her to continue working on his yard for the summer.

Osami: I earned $4.75 an hour working for the landscaping company, and our customers were charged $10 an hour. Because I'll be providing my own transportation and equipment, I think $8 an hour would be a fair price.

Mr. Kincaid: I was thinking $6.50 would be reasonable. Since you're working on your own, you won't have many of the expenses of running a business. And, the person who takes care of our neighbor's yard does it for $6 an hour.

Osami: Well, I could probably do your yard work for $7.75 an hour, but I will have a number of extra expenses. I'll need to pay for gas, lawn mower maintenance, and plant supplies.

Mr. Kincaid: I hadn't thought of that. Still, the fellow who does the neighbor's yard charges only $6 to do the same kind of work.

Osami: That might be. But ask your neighbor what happened to her roses after they were pruned incorrectly. I think my experience is worth a little more. I've had two summers of experience working at a landscaping company, and I've completed training programs on plant disease, drainage, and maintenance.

Mr. Kincaid: I know you're experienced, and I want you to keep my yard looking as great as it looks now. Come to think of it, you're always done in about three hours, and that other fellow usually takes four hours to do my neighbor's yard. If I consider your experience, perhaps $7.75 an hour is a fair price.

 Osami began the negotiation by asking for $8 an hour. What did she use as a standard to come up with that rate? What was Mr. Kincaid using as a standard when he offered $6 an hour? What convinced Mr. Kincaid that his original offer was not fair? What standard did he wind up using? Did both Osami and Mr. Kincaid come to the conclusion that $7.75 was a fair hourly wage? Why do you say so?

_____

_____

_____

_____

PRACTICE

1. With a partner, prepare a short role-play depicting a conflict. After the role-play, ask the audience to recommend methods to help settle the dispute. Be prepared to decide how you would resolve the conflict.

2. In small groups, use the Internet to find information about negotiating salary increases with supervisors. Present your information in the form of "tips" for employees. Make sure your tips include fair solutions for employees *and* companies. Try to show how seeing a supervisor's perspective can help employees during the salary negotiating process.

3. Abraham Lincoln, the 16th U.S. President, said, "When I'm getting ready to reason with a man, I spend one-third of my time thinking about myself and what I am going to say, and two-thirds thinking about him and what he is going to say." In a one-page reflection paper, explain what he meant by that quote and relate it to what you've learned in this workshop.

> *All is fair in love and war.*
>
> —Traditional proverb

SUMMARY

➤ When negotiating an agreement, it is essential to think of solutions that would be acceptable to you if you were on the other side of the bargaining table.

➤ Creative negotiating involves focusing on interests instead of positions, and brainstorming to find as many solutions as possible.

➤ Brainstorming, which usually involves at least two people, is a strategy for setting our imaginations free to think of all possible resolutions, no matter how foolish they might seem at the time.

➤ To ensure your negotiations are fair, ask for what is fair, establish your standards of fairness, and be open to the other side's standards.

1. Why is it unwise to use "either-or" or "splitting it down the middle" solutions?

_____

_____

_____

2. Why is focusing on underlying interests critical when inventing solutions?

_____

_____

_____

3. How do you "brainstorm"? How is it used in negotiation?

_____

_____

_____

4. Why do you think being open to the other side's standards of fairness is important in negotiation?

_____

_____

_____

5. Briefly summarize a conflict you're involved in and brainstorm three solutions.

_____

_____

_____

1. Use the Internet or your library to find an account of the feuding Hatfields and McCoys. As you read about these two families, try to determine the cause of their conflict and why it continued for so many years. Write a short paper offering creative suggestions for ways that it might have been resolved.

2. Identify a current news story about an ongoing negotiation. The negotiation may involve the purchase of a business, the trade of a professional athlete from one team to another, or a labor contract between a company and its unionized employees. Imagine that both sides have asked you to work with them to negotiate a fair solution to their problem. Your job is to study the situation by researching the story in the media (newspapers, magazines, Internet, radio programs, and TV news programs) and by preparing a "Negotiation Fairness Brief" that includes the following three parts.

   • A brief summary of the problem; a description of all sides involved in the problem (there may be more than two sides); and a summary of the progress (or lack of progress) in the negotiation from when it began up to the present date.

   • A description of each side's apparent standard of fairness, using examples from the materials you have obtained in your research.

   • A proposal of a solution that would be fair to all sides.

Determining whether or not a solution is fair can be very difficult, for what is fair often depends on circumstances and opinions.

51

⟳ Discover the skills required for effective intervention in conflicts.

⟳ Learn the process of mediation.

⟳ Identify situations that lend themselves to informal mediation.

©2001 PhotoDisc, Inc.

KEEPING THE PEACE

For causes that seem trivial, two of your coworkers are involved in an ongoing quarrel, building up more resentment against each other every day. Your family has been bickering about little things since the weekend, and no one in the house can get any peace. Sometimes, help from an impartial third party is the best way to resolve conflicts. This workshop demonstrates the value of the peacemaker in conflicts and the skills necessary for effective formal and informal mediation.

One Bad Apple . . .

Sharif, Luis, and Lianne—members of the Diversity Task Force—met for lunch to discuss Albert, the fourth team member.

Lianne: Albert can't work with anybody, and he won't consider our ideas.

Sharif: At the last meeting, I really wanted to let him have it!

Luis: Maybe he has personal issues.

Lianne: Well, he's hindering our objectives. I say we ignore him.

Luis: That won't help. Let's find out what's up with him.

Lianne: Oh, all right. Some of his ideas are good. I'll talk to him quietly before the next meeting. I'll say we value his ideas, but feel that he doesn't value ours.

✔ *What other peacemaking strategies could Sharif, Luis, and Lianne use?*

TOOLS OF THE TRADE

The Advantages of Mediation

When two parties in a dispute formally agree to have a third party help them resolve their differences, that process is called *mediation*. Not all conflicts require a mediator, or peacemaker. When conflicts are deadlocked, unfocused, drawn-out, and hindered by a lack of understanding, mediation may be the best—and only—solution.

➤ Mediation helps the two parties communicate.

➤ Mediation identifies solutions that the parties might not have discovered on their own.

➤ Mediation can reduce emotional flare-ups by giving both parties a chance to express their views.

➤ Mediation preserves both parties' self-respect, so that neither party feels they have lost, regardless of the outcome.

Qualities of a Good Mediator

Not everyone is cut out to be a mediator. Mediators must be able to remove themselves from either side. The following traits are must-haves for successful mediators.

➤ Respect for others

➤ Impartiality

➤ Patience

➤ Decisiveness

➤ Firmness

➤ Analytical mind

➤ Creativity

➤ Trustworthiness

➤ Good communication skills

Formal and Informal Mediation

Most of the time, mediation occurs in an informal manner. In serious workplace or government conflicts, however, a more formal approach must be taken. Remember, before someone can help mediate, both parties must agree to the mediation.

➤ **Formal mediation.** In a large firm or government agency, a supervisor may issue a referral that sends the disputing parties to professionals with specific training in the arts of mediation.

➤ **Informal mediation.** Informal types of mediation are the ones you are most likely to experience. For example, two people who have been arguing may call on a third person to help settle the issue. Or, perhaps the third party volunteers to help.

➤ **Arbitration.** It's important to remember that a mediator is not an arbitrator. An arbitrator is someone who is empowered to make a judgment in the case—and the parties must accept the ruling.

Mediation Checklist

A mediator's precise role varies according to the situation. Typically, however, in both formal and informal mediation, the mediator:

1. Meets with the parties both individually and jointly to hear their views.

2. Arranges meetings between the parties in settings that maximize the chances for effective communication (for example, a quiet chat over lunch, as opposed to a highly charged staff meeting with other people involved).

3. Establishes priorities (for example, "First, let's figure out why you disagreed so much about Project A").

4. Identifies and clarifies the areas of dispute for both parties.

5. Suggests possible solutions and stimulates the parties to suggest others.

6. Helps both parties discuss the merits of the potential solutions.

7. Nudges the parties toward adopting a mutually acceptable solution.

8. Helps define a clear plan for future action by both parties.

Mediation Ground Rules

In addition to the mediator's major goal—helping the parties find a resolution—he or she must also facilitate positive, constructive communication.

1. Only let one person speak at a time.

2. Force the parties to attack the problem, *not* the person.

3. Make it clear that things said in the room stay in the room.

4. Require the parties to listen and tell the truth.

When conflicts are deadlocked, unfocused, drawn-out, and hindered by a lack of understanding, mediation may be the best—and only—solution.

©2001 PhotoDisc, Inc.

THE PEACEMAKER
Segment 4

Here's your chance to practice mediation. In the first segment of this video, you'll observe a mediator's attempts to facilitate an informal negotiation between two coworkers, Pam and Josh. As you watch the conflict unfold, try to think of what you would do as the mediator. Then, you'll meet Rae and Sandy, and be asked to help mediate their conflict. Valerie Barnett joins us again to comment on the importance of listening, mutually satisfying resolutions, and exploring new solutions.

> " *When you come to a road-block, take a detour.* "
>
> —Mary Kay Ash

Rae asks Sandy to give up her Saturday.

Post-Viewing Questions

1. How would you mediate the dispute between Pam and Josh?

_____

_____

_____

2. What solution would satisfy both Sandy and Rae?

_____

_____

_____

Peace-ing It Together

Tony and Deena, two nurses at the health clinic, just couldn't seem to get along with each other. I'm not their supervisor, Dieu thought, so what can I do about it?

Today, however, Dieu sees that their disagreements are affecting their work. After taking a patient's history, Deena sets the patient's chart on a counter for the doctor to pick up. "Excuse me," she says with exaggerated politeness as she passes close to Tony, who is sorting through other files at the same counter. A moment later, Tony plops a stack of folders on top of Deena's chart, burying it.

"Wait," Dieu says, "There's a new chart under there. Deena just put it down."

Tony points a finger at another counter across the hall and says, "Charts waiting for the doctors belong there. But Ms. Efficiency always knows a better way, doesn't she?"

Dieu digs the new chart out of the pile and moves it across the hall. "Hey Tony," she says, "it's not a big deal, okay? We can put the charts wherever you like. But I'm worried about this friction between you two."

"Talk to her about it," Tony snaps.

"Okay, I will," Dieu says, "but is there any way I could help? I know you care about doing things right, so I'm sure you don't want these little disagreements to interfere with the rest of the staff and the patients. Let's talk about it later, okay?"

Dieu also speaks with Deena, who seems to be harboring similar hostilities. When Dieu sees Tony again, she says she wants to take him and Deena to lunch at the local diner.

"My treat," Dieu says. "The one condition is that you must be nice to each other. And maybe we'll talk about what's really bothering you."

Tony grimaces, but agrees.

 In groups of three, role-play Dieu mediating the discussion between Deena and Tony. Others in the class should comment on the exchanges that occur and the use of the "Mediation Checklist."

PRACTICE

1. Reflect on conflict situations where you acted as an informal mediator. How were you drawn into the conflict as a mediator? How did you feel? How did the quarreling parties deal with the conflict? Based on your experiences, can you think of any additional qualities that a good mediator must possess? List any additional qualities on a piece of paper, and be prepared to share your list and your experiences with the class.

2. Continue to practice mediation strategies by dividing into small groups. Set up a role-play exercise based on a work situation common to your group's experiences. Have one person try to mediate a dispute involving two or more others. Be prepared to present your skit to the class.

3. In an effort to reduce school violence, many schools have set up programs in which students serve as mediators for conflicts involving other students. Using an Internet search engine, enter the phrase "peer mediation" and explore some of the school sites you find. Share your findings with the class.

> *A good mediator tries to determine the true intentions of each party and communicate them to the other.*
>
> —Judith R. Gordon

SUMMARY

➤ When two parties in a dispute formally agree to have a third party help them resolve their differences, the process is called mediation.

➤ When conflicts are deadlocked, unfocused, drawn-out, and hindered by a lack of understanding, mediation may be the best—and only—solution.

➤ In addition to the mediator's major goal—helping the parties find a resolution—he or she must also facilitate positive, constructive communication.

➤ Unlike mediators, arbitrators are empowered to make judgments in the case, and the quarreling parties must accept the ruling.

1. What does a mediator do?

_____

_____

_____

2. List some advantages of mediation.

_____

_____

_____

3. Describe the difference between mediators and arbitrators.

_____

_____

_____

4. List and compare your personal qualities with "Qualities of a Good Mediator." Would you be a good or bad mediator? Why?

_____

_____

_____

> *Just remember, there's a right way and a wrong way to do everything and the wrong way is to keep trying to make everybody else do it the right way.*
>
> —Colonel Potter, M*A*S*H

PROJECTS

1. Visit a large business, and ask them about their mediation procedures. Who helps in the mediation process? How do employees access the mediation process? How often is the process used, and how effective is it? Write and submit a short report of your findings.

2. Recall a recent time when you were "caught in the middle" between two disputing friends or coworkers. Outline an effective mediation process you could have used to help the people reach a resolution to their conflict. Remember to use anger management skills and the "Mediation Checklist." Develop a script as if you were "rewriting" the situation, using what you've learned in this workshop.

The Nobel Peace Prize and Nobel Institute

What do Mother Teresa, Martin Luther King, Jr., and the Dalai Lama all have in common? Each has won the Nobel Peace Prize, an award given annually since 1901 by the Nobel Committee in Oslo, Norway. Peace is one of five areas mentioned in the will of Alfred Nobel, a successful Swedish businessman and inventor who left his fortune to create the Nobel prizes in literature, medicine, physics, chemistry, and peace. A sixth prize in economics was added in 1968.

In his will, Alfred Nobel (1833-1896) stated that the prizes be given to those who, during the preceding year, "shall have conferred the greatest benefit on mankind" and that one prize be given to the person who "shall have done the most or the best work for the fraternity between nations, for the abolition or reduction of standing armies and for the holding and promotion of peace congresses." The Nobel Peace Prize is one of the world's highest honors and is awarded each year on December 10 at the Norwegian Nobel Institute. The Institute was established in 1904 and assists the Nobel Committee in selecting the recipient of the Nobel Peace in addition to organizing the annual Nobel events in Oslo.

The selection process for the Nobel Peace Prize is a long one. Present and past members of the Nobel Committee and advisors at the Nobel Institute typically make nominations for candidates. Others such as university professors in law, political science, history and philosophy; government officials; and international organizations also nominate candidates. The Nobel Peace Prize can be divided between no more than three laureates; however, it often goes to single individuals. It is customary for Nobel Peace Prize winners to give a speech at the awarding ceremony. To learn more about past winners of the Nobel Peace Prize and read their speeches, visit the Nobel e-museum at www.nobel.no.

GOALS

→ Understand the difference between negotiating face-to-face and electronically.

→ Learn the importance of avoiding anger, humor, and irony in e-mail messages.

©2001 PhotoDisc, Inc.

A GESTURE PAINTS A THOUSAND WORDS

Much of what we express is tied to nonverbal behavior—the tone of our voice, facial expressions, gestures, and body language. Our meanings are so ingrained in nonverbal communication, that we often communicate poorly when we have to rely on words alone. Because businesses increasingly rely on communicating with customers and coworkers at a distance, today's negotiation strategies should be refined to meet the challenges of electronic communication. This workshop focuses on the fine points of negotiations over e-mail, with an eye on what to do—and what to avoid.

Friend or Foe?

A.J. is about to introduce his plans for the new project to Jodie, the project leader. A.J. and Jodie—who have never met—are located in regional offices 200 miles apart. Because lack of time and money will not allow them to meet face-to-face, A.J. communicates with Jodie by e-mail.

A.J. e-mails the detailed outline of his plan, followed by a brief introduction of himself. Jodie is impressed with A.J.'s plan, and finds his ambition noble. She e-mails A.J. back, saying: "You're crazy if you think that will work! No one is that good!" She laughs good-naturedly as she clicks "Send."

✔ *How do you think A.J. responded? Where did Jodie go wrong?*

TOOLS OF THE TRADE

"Netiquette" and Negotiating

The same rules that apply to professional e-mail correspondence are especially important for electronic negotiations.

➤ **Avoid sending messages expressing anger, humor, or irony.** Angry messages should *always* be avoided, especially when trying to resolve conflicts. Because humor and irony often depend on facial expressions and tone of voice, their intent is often lost and misunderstood in written messages.

➤ **Assume your message is as permanent as a letter or a memo.** An e-mail you send to someone on your team regarding your position or strategy might get into the wrong hands. It could even be admitted as evidence in a lawsuit.

➤ **Use appropriate language.** Don't use profanity or make derogatory comments about racial, ethnic, or religious groups, even as an attempt to put the other side at ease. Your joke may backfire if perceived as insulting.

➤ **Don't use capital letters to make a point.** In written messages, capital letters are the equivalent of shouting. Appearing calm during negotiations is vital to reaching a friendly agreement.

Key Ideas

★ **nonverbal behavior—** methods of communicating without spoken language

★ **netiquette—** network etiquette, the correct way to conduct yourself when you're communicating online or on a computer network

Today's negotiation strategies should be refined to meet the challenges of electronic communication.

©2001 PhotoDisc, Inc.

WHEN YOU ONLY HAVE YOUR E-WORDS

Most of the negotiations that you experience will probably take place in face-to-face interactions. You and the "other side" may meet in the hallway, in an office, or in the cafeteria to discuss your differences. As you negotiate, each of you can immediately respond to what the other side says. You can also consider nonverbal forms of communication—tone of voice and facial expression. Two-way communication makes it easier for you to sense such things as whether you have been misunderstood and whether the other side's "final offer" is *really* the final offer.

But what if you can't meet face-to-face to resolve your conflict? What if you can only communicate with the "other side" through the cyberwaves? In the workplace, people are increasingly communicating electronically—using faxes, modems, and e-mail. Conflict can occur in these situations too.

Unlike face-to-face discussions, many forms of electronic communication allow only one-way communication. The receiver of a message often cannot respond immediately. Furthermore, depending on the form of communication, the receiver may not be able to see facial expressions or hear other side's tone of voice.

When you communicate over the phone or by voice mail, you cannot see the person on the other end of the line, and that person can't see you. When you send a message through e-mail or by fax, you and the recipient of your message cannot see *or* hear each other. In all of these cases, nonverbal cues are either limited or nonexistent.

Think about how your responses have been affected by one-way communication. Then, re-read "Friend or Foe?" and rewrite Jodie's response to A.J. based on what you've learned about the limits of e-mail correspondence.

> *The difference between the right word and the almost right word is the difference between lightning and the lightning bug.*
>
> —Mark Twain

Two Days

Anesa has been working with Jesse on a rush job for a client since last Friday. Jesse works out of the regional office, which is in a different time zone, and Anesa works at company headquarters. Because they also have different working hours, Anesa can only reach Jesse by phone from 10 a.m. to 2 p.m., her time. As a result, they mostly communicate through e-mail. When Anesa arrives at work Monday morning—two days before the deadline for the job— she finds the following e-mail posted to her address:

> Anesa,
>
> There's no way we can meet the deadline now, THANKS TO YOU. I would have worked all weekend if YOU had sent the Simmons file like you said you would.
>
> But that's just like you guys at headquarters. If it doesn't affect your paycheck, YOU DON'T GIVE A RIP whether we can meet our clients' deadlines.
>
> At least if I make a promise, I keep it. DO send the Simmons file when you can fit it into your busy schedule!
>
> Jesse

> *Man does not live by words alone, despite the fact that sometimes he has to eat them.*
>
> —Adlai Stevenson, statesman

Jesse and Anesa must resolve this conflict if they are going to meet the deadline.

 With a partner, take over Anesa and Jesse's negotiation over e-mail. (If you don't have access to e-mail in class, write scripts back and forth to each other.) Keep negotiating until the conflict is resolved. Remember to use the negotiation techniques you've learned from earlier workshops.

1. Send an e-mail to a member of your class, intentionally breaking several of the "netiquette" rules. Print a hard copy of your e-mail and write down what you intended to convey. After the recipient views the message, ask what he or she thought you were trying to convey, including the emotional intent. Compare information and share it with the class.

2. Did you know that 500 of the most commonly used words in the English language have over 14,000 definitions? In small groups, make a list of at least 25 words that could cause conflict or be entirely misunderstood. How could some of these words be misinterpreted in e-mail negotiations?

3. With a partner, use at least five of your words from exercise #2 in an e-mail negotiation depicting the confusion and misunderstanding that can result from people assuming incorrect definitions. Be prepared to present your negotiation for the class.

> *If the word has the potency to revive and make us free, it also has the power to bind, imprison, and destroy.*
>
> —Ralph Ellison, writer

SUMMARY

➤ Today's negotiation strategies should be refined to meet the challenges of electronic communication.

➤ The same rules that apply to professional e-mail correspondence are especially important for electronic negotiations.

➤ Angry messages should always be avoided, especially when trying to resolve conflicts. Because humor and irony often depend on facial expressions and tone of voice, their intent is often lost and misunderstood in written messages.

1. What is the major difference between negotiating face-to-face and negotiating by e-mail?

_____

_____

2. Why should you avoid using anger, humor, or irony in e-mail negotiations?

_____

_____

3. What are some useful communication techniques to use when negotiating by e-mail?

_____

_____

PROJECTS

1. Using the Internet or a library, research lawsuits related to e-mail and other forms of electronic communication. Is electronic communication as valid in a court of law as a written document? What allowance does the law make for the fact that e-mail is not signed by hand? Can a message be sent through your e-mail account without your permission? Report your findings to the class.

2. Want to solve the problems of the world—online? Virtual United Nations Web sites are great places to practice negotiating at a distance. Designed to simulate the structure and format of the real United Nations (UN), model UN groups let everyday people role-play the positions and beliefs of governments around the globe. Visit a model UN Web site (www.unol.org is a good place to start) and follow the chain of arguments on one topic. Analyze the participants' online negotiating skills based on what you've learned in this workshop. How does the lack of nonverbal cues contribute to the difficulty? If you like, submit an intelligent position of your own. Report your experiences to the class.

THE BOILING POINT

GOALS

→ Identify appropriate and inappropriate conflict-related behavior.

→ Discover steps to take when conflict reaches the "boiling point."

→ Identify conflicts that may warrant "in-house" or legal remedies.

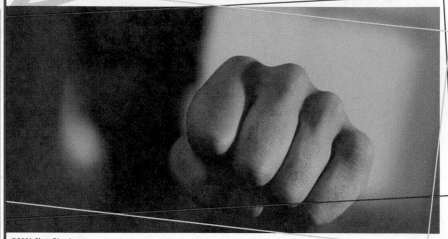

©2001 PhotoDisc, Inc.

LOSING YOUR COOL

Think about the last time you were angry. Did your anger make you blind to resolutions? Anger can be positive. It can focus your attention, bring negative feelings out in the open, and warn others that you mean business. Uncontrolled anger, however, can cause you to say unwise things, make exaggerated accusations, and harm yourself or others. This workshop identifies appropriate conflict-related behavior, presents "in-house" remedies for managing unresolved conflicts, and focuses on methods for dealing with anger when it reaches the boiling point.

The Last Straw

Ruby stared at the kitchen stockroom and blinked. The diner's manager for 22 years, she'd never worked with such an incompetent staff. After being short on eggs last Saturday and napkins the week before, her patience had worn thin. As she counted the inventory, she noticed 20 boxes of straws, and 2 pounds of potatoes. "No! No! No! I specifically asked those girls to order 2 boxes of straws and 20 pounds of potatoes!!"

"We need 10 hashbrown orders on table 21," a waitress called to the cook.

"Oh, I'll handle THAT!!" Ruby yelled, storming out with a box of straws. "I'M SORRY, DID YOU ORDER POTATOES?" she screamed as she emptied the box of straws onto the customers' table.

✔ **How should the cook and the waitresses react to Ruby's outburst?**

TOOLS OF THE TRADE

When Anger Reaches the "Boiling Point"

What should you do when conflict reaches the "boiling point"? When a conflict arises, and one or both of the disputants are angry, that anger is going to be counterproductive to the negotiation process. Learn to manage your anger *and* the anger of others by practicing the following tips from Workshop 4.

➤ **Accept the fact that you're angry.** Acknowledge your responsibility for dealing with the emotion.

➤ **Decide exactly what you're angry about.** Analyze the source of your feelings, and separate the real problem from insignificant matters. Identify deep emotions underlying the surface problem.

➤ **Be sure you understand the facts of the situation.** Confirm the facts; don't waste energy being angry about a misunderstanding.

➤ **Find someone to speak to about the problem.** The best person to address is the one at whom you're angry. If that is not possible, choose a neutral party whom you trust to give good advice.

➤ **When you speak up, do it in an assertive—not aggressive—manner.** Use constructive advice skills. Describe the problem objectively, describe your feelings, describe your needs and desires, and focus on the goal you want to achieve.

➤ **Propose a solution.** Find a resolution that is acceptable to you and potentially acceptable to the other person.

➤ **Reflect on the experience and learn from it.** Think about whether you managed your anger in the best possible way. Then decide whether you should modify your approach in the future.

Key Ideas

★ **accountability**—taking responsibility for your choices and their results

★ **arbitration**—the process of settling a dispute between two or more parties by an unbiased third party

★ **conflict**—a sharp disagreement over interests or ideas

★ **stress**—mental or physical tension or strain

On the Net

Sometimes legal remedies are the only way to solve disputes between companies and their employees. This Web site provides useful tools and resources, including a legal dictionary and advice under the "How We Can Help You" section. Learn more about today's most common legal problems in the workplace at:

www.uslaw.com/employment

In-House Solutions, Arbitration, and Legal Action

When conflicts occur in the workplace, ideally, the people involved in the conflict are able to resolve their differences quickly and peaceably. However, if the conflict continues, other action is often taken.

➤ **IN-HOUSE SOLUTIONS**

An "in-house" company remedy can be a fair and efficient way to resolve workplace conflicts. In these situations, the company relies on the formal process of disciplinary action outlined in the employee handbook, which generally involves the following four steps.

Step 1: Oral warning. The employees involved are approached and warned of the consequences of continued conflict behaviors.

Step 2: Written warning. If the situation does not improve, a written warning is issued.

Step 3: Disciplinary probation. If the problem still persists, another document is written that establishes a time period during which the situation has to be resolved. During the disciplinary probation, those involved are monitored closely.

Step 4: Termination or reinstatement. When the disciplinary probation period is completed, those involved are either reinstated back to full status or terminated, depending on their behavior.

➤ **ARBITRATION**

Often, a mediator will be brought in to assist the negotiation process. After both sides have aired their perception of the discrepancy, this person helps the parties come up with creative solutions that are agreeable to all. If it seems unlikely that the parties can come to an agreement, both sides may agree to use an arbitrator. Unlike a mediator, the arbitrator gathers all information and makes a decision that both parties must accept.

➤ **LEGAL ACTION**

Some conflicts may warrant legal remedies. These conflicts usually involve harassment, discrimination, or unsafe working conditions. Lawsuits are filed, and conflicts are resolved through the legal process.

An eye for eye only ends up making the whole world blind.

—Mahatma Gandhi

Accountable and Unaccountable Behaviors

Some conflicts can never be negotiated or resolved simply because people are not willing to be accountable for their actions. People who are accountable take ownership for their actions. They accept blame *and* enjoy the rewards for their decisions. They don't make excuses or disappear when a mistake is discovered. Exhibiting behaviors that are dominating, dismissive, inhibiting, negative, blocking, or competitive will stand in the way of conflict resolution.

UNACCOUNTABLE PEOPLE	ACCOUNTABLE PEOPLE
Blame others.	Accept responsibility.
Back away from accepting fault for problems.	Step forward to accept fault for problems.
Cover up mistakes.	Admit to mistakes.
Hide the problem.	Confront the problem.
Make excuses.	Deal with failure.
Pass corrections to others.	Fix what is wrong.
Disown poor results.	Own both good and poor results.

PAST THE BOILING POINT

Workplace violence—an extreme expression of anger and aggression—is a growing concern. According to the National Institute of Occupational Safety and Health:

- Homicide is the second leading cause of death on the job. Among women, it is the number-one cause of workplace death.

- On average, 20 workers are murdered every week in the United States.

- About 18,000 U.S. workers are the victims of assault each week.

Much of this violence stems from interactions with the public (for instance, hold-ups at convenience stores) rather than from conflicts between coworkers. Still, in the wake of horrific new reports, there is more and more worry about disgruntled employees erupting into violence.

 Using the Internet, newspapers, or magazines, research at least three occurrences of workplace violence. Develop a checklist of actions to take when conflict passes the boiling point.

Ingrid works as an accountant for a large financial invest-ment firm. One day, her manager paired her up with a new coworker, Maria, to handle the accounts of a major client.

Ingrid and Maria had problems immediately. In their daily meetings, Maria not only dom-inated the conversation and decision-making, but she refused to listen attentively to Ingrid's suggestions and concerns. Maria was certain that her ideas were always right. Yet when her decisions turned out to be poor ones, she laid the blame on Ingrid.

This infuriated Ingrid, who began spreading rumors about how Maria was an arrogant and difficult person. Soon enough, everyone in the firm was aware of the conflict, and it began to affect employee morale negatively.

After two months, neither Ingrid nor Maria attempted to resolve their differences. Each of them was seething with anger towards the other, and their manager was not aware of the situation. Maria began interrupting Ingrid increasingly during meetings, which caused Ingrid to walk out once without a word. Then, during an important meeting that included their client, Maria made a negative remark about Ingrid's work. Ingrid exploded in anger and proceeded to yell at Maria. The meeting ended abruptly, and later that week, so too did business with their client.

Got It Right

Andy and Jason work as assistant chefs in a busy three-star restaurant. Their duties include preparing salads and deserts before the dinner rush, helping waiters with their orders, and assist-ing the head chef to make everything run smoothly in the kitchen.

Andy and Jason have never gotten along very well. They have worked together for a year, and Andy feels Jason doesn't carry his share of the workload. For example, Jason frequently arrives to work 15 to 30 minutes late. By this time, Andy has already begun preparation work, and the manager and head chef are rarely around to notice. Jason also has occasional lapses in the presentation of his food. When complaints come back to the kitchen, both Andy and Jason take the blame.

One day, Andy decided to confront Jason and asked him if he wanted to go out after work. Jason agreed, and over a couple of games of darts Andy expressed his irritation with some of Jason's work habits. Jason took Andy's concerns in stride, and, not want-ing to lose his job or cause any further problems, told Andy that he would be more con-scientious about his responsibilities at work.

Jason had been totally unaware of Andy's frustration with him. Once Andy raised the issue, the two promising chefs began working well together.

The Unfriendly Skies

Louis and Juan sit down at the union meeting, eager to discuss the airline ticket agents' current problem. Since the change in flight schedules, the agents have been overwhelmed with long lines of people checking in. The passengers have been getting upset, and the agents have grown frazzled and dissatisfied.

Drummond, the union representative, begins with routine matters. Louis gestures for attention, but Drummond calls on Juan instead.

Juan: Lately we've been having some trouble handling the workload. The lines are getting too long. We're issuing tickets and checking baggage as fast as we can, but the passengers are upset about it.

Drummond: What's the problem? The number of passengers hasn't increased, so why can't you keep up?

Louis: Oh come off it, man! Pay some attention to what's going on here! The new schedules are impossible—you're clumping flights together at one o'clock and three o'clock! I'm so tired of this garbage!

Drummond: *(stiffens)* As your union representative, I do pay attention.

Juan: Look, Mr. Drummond, we don't mean to criticize you. We're just saying that the work conditions have changed, and we're unhappy about it. We feel that, as our representative, you could speak to management.

Louis: Tell those idiots they need to do something! Or we'll all quit!

Drummond: *(frowns and mutters)* Management doesn't respond well to griping.

Louis: *(slams his fist on the table)* WHOSE SIDE ARE YOU ON?

Drummond gets up. Juan pleads with his eyes and gestures for him to stay.

Juan: Mr. Drummond, it's not just a gripe, because it's in management's interests to keep travelers happy. If a supervisor could help out behind the counter at busy times, it'd make a big difference for us and for the passengers.

Drummond: *(concedes)* All right. I'll see what I can do.

> "An angry man opens his mouth and shuts up his eyes."
>
> —Cato

Contrast Juan's and Louis' conflict resolution techniques. Why does Juan get better results?

71

1. With a partner, create two role-plays for resolving a conflict at work. Use an unaccountable behavior for the first role-play, and the corresponding accountable behavior for the second role-play. Note differences in outcomes in a two-column chart.

2. Describe, in one or two paragraphs, a recent example of a conflict that reached the boiling point. Describe your role, what occurred, and the current status of the conflict. Then, discuss how an arbitrator might resolve the conflict.

3. Using the Internet, discover some additional ways to manage your anger. Be prepared to share your findings with a poster or PowerPoint slide presentation. Some sites to try follow.

   • http://www.angermgmt.com/

   • http://www.plainsense.com/health/Stress/

We cannot learn from one another until we stop shouting at one another—until we speak quietly enough so that our words can be heard as well as our voices.

—Richard Nixon, 37th U.S. President

SUMMARY

➤ Uncontrolled anger is a barrier to conflict resolution.

➤ Some conflicts can never be negotiated or resolved simply because people are not willing to be accountable for their actions.

➤ Accountable people have self-esteem, confidence, and courage.

➤ An "in-house" company remedy can be a fair and efficient way to resolve workplace conflicts.

➤ If it seems unlikely that quarreling parties can come to an agreement, both sides may agree to use an arbitrator.

➤ Conflicts that involve harassment, discrimination, or unsafe working conditions may warrant legal remedies.

REVIEW QUESTIONS

1. What is an "in-house" solution?

   _____

   _____

2. What are some positive outcomes of anger?

   _____

   _____

3. What are some options to take when a conflict reaches the boiling point?

   _____

   _____

PROJECTS

1. Interview several supervisors of businesses in your community. Ask them to describe the kinds of conflicts that have led to disciplinary action. Design a flowchart that outlines the sequence of events that led to the disciplinary action, the steps that were taken by the company, and any consequences for the employee(s). Present your findings to the class.

2. For one week, keep a journal, documenting situations where people get angry. (You can document instances of your own anger, if applicable.) List the steps taken, if any, to manage anger. Also note any behaviors that were counterproductive to finding a resolution. Present your findings in a report.

3. Research the necessary steps to take when conflict makes for an unsafe workplace. Write a report outlining the steps, and include a flowchart visual.

GOALS

➜ Discover company policies used to solve problems.

➜ Learn the typical steps in formal disciplinary procedures.

➜ Identify situations which lend themselves to formal discipline.

©2001 PhotoDisc, Inc.

HOUSE RULES

What would it be like to play a game of Monopoly without rules? No one rolls the dice, or takes turns. Money and properties are up for grabs. Though no one claims to like rules, they are essential for easing operations and solving conflicts. In the workplace, company policies help employees understand the expectations of the company and the consequences of not meeting those expectations. A company's disciplinary action policy can be the best point of reference when problems arise. This workshop focuses on how businesses use disciplinary policies to solve conflicts in the workplace.

Following Suit

Martin loved the new company policy that allowed employees to dress casually on Fridays. Putting on his old blue jeans or sweats was a great break from wearing a suit and tie Monday through Thursday.

One Friday, Martin's supervisor, Patrice, called him into her office. When Martin arrived in Patrice's office, he was surprised to find that he was being given a written warning about his Friday attire.

"Martin, I'm disappointed with your abuse of our Friday casual dress policy," Patrice said. "It clearly states that sweat pants and jeans with holes are not allowed."

Martin gulped. He had assumed that "casual" meant "casual"—and didn't bother to read the policy.

 Was Patrice right to give Martin a written warning?

TOOLS OF THE TRADE

Common Company Policies

Problems in the workplace come in various kinds and degrees. They can be as slight as employee violations of break times to serious infractions such as employee theft of company secrets. Company policies are created to serve as control devices for standards of behavior.

The following policies are shared by most companies. In addition to these, specific policies are created for particular businesses or departments. For example, a policy about customer courtesy for retail businesses would be applicable to the employees who work directly with customers.

- ➤ Attendance
- ➤ Dress code
- ➤ Tardiness
- ➤ Safety
- ➤ Breaks
- ➤ Smoking/drugs/alcohol use
- ➤ Job expectations
- ➤ Company property
- ➤ Payroll/time sheets or time cards
- ➤ Conduct

Offenses That Lead to Disciplinary Action

Company policies are typically described in employee handbooks, and information is provided during orientation sessions at the time of employment. The following list illustrates some offenses that can lead to disciplinary action in business, industrial, and other organizations. Some of the offenses require further explanation by individual companies. For example, what is meant by "excessive absence" and "repeated tardiness" needs to be defined so that employees and supervisors know what standards are being applied.

- ➤ Dishonesty, deception, or fraud, including computer fraud
- ➤ Theft of property, including trade secrets
- ➤ Sleeping on the job
- ➤ Repeated tardiness
- ➤ Failure to report injuries
- ➤ Excessive absence
- ➤ Failure to meet quality or quantity standards
- ➤ Leaving work without permission
- ➤ Safety-rule violation
- ➤ Alcohol or drug abuse
- ➤ Use of abusive language or threatening language
- ➤ Possession of liquor or illegal drugs
- ➤ Gambling
- ➤ Discourtesy to customers
- ➤ Insubordination
- ➤ Willful damage to property
- ➤ Carrying concealed weapons
- ➤ Sexual harassment
- ➤ Fighting
- ➤ Age, racial, or national origin harassment
- ➤ Horseplay
- ➤ Violation of grooming or dress code
- ➤ Working for a competitor

Key Ideas

- ★ **policy**—a pre-established regulation for dealing with an issue or a problem
- ★ **disciplinary action**—penalty or punishment associated with violation of a rule
- ★ **probation**—trial period during which a worker is given time to correct performance problems

75

Common Disciplinary Processes

When an employee violates company regulations, most policies are designed to "let the punishment fit the crime." Few violations are considered serious enough to warrant immediate discharge. Those violations might include theft, falsifying employment applications or work records, possession of illegal drugs or weapons, divulging trade secrets, physical assault, or deliberate damage to material or property.

Less serious offenses may not warrant discharge the first time, but repeated offenses may. Disciplinary policies generally allow enough time for employees to make necessary adjustments to workplace behaviors.

Penalties for violations of less serious infractions include:

➤ **Oral or written warnings**—notices that a more severe penalty (frequently specified) will be applied at the next infraction of a policy

➤ **Demotion**—a reduction in job responsibilities, usually accompanied by a reduction in hourly pay or salary

➤ **Disciplinary layoff**—a temporary separation from the organization and payroll, typically for a few days or weeks

➤ **Docking of pay**—loss of pay for time missed (generally applies to absenteeism or chronic tardiness)

Progressive Discipline

Many businesses find that the use of progressive discipline is effective for producing positive outcomes. When a company applies progressive discipline, the level of punishment is increased each time an employee commits an infraction.

A possible disciplinary progression sequence follows:

➤ **Step 1: Written warning.** The employee involved is approached and warned of the consequences of continued conflict behaviors.

➤ **Step 2: Disciplinary probation.** If the problem still persists, another document is written that establishes a time period during which the situation has to be resolved. During the disciplinary probation, the employee is monitored closely.

➤ **Step 3: Decision-making leave.** The employee is placed on a one-day, paid leave. He or she is instructed to think about his or her commitment to the organization and to solving the problem. Upon return, if the employee has elected to stay, he or she immediately meets with the supervisor to set specific performance goals and to develop a plan of action.

➤ **Step 4: Termination.** If the employee fails to meet the expectations outlined after the decision-making leave, termination results.

CHRIS SCHRADER, VICE PRESIDENT, HUMAN RESOURCES: COMPANY POLICIES
Segment 5

In this program, you will meet Chris Schrader, vice president of human resources for InterArt, a Hallmark company. During the video, Chris provides a perspective from the management side of problem solving and explains how company policy helps avoid and resolve problems. Chris also discusses problems and conflicts that arise from absenteeism, job performance, and behavior. As you watch the video, think about the role of company rules and polices in resolving and preventing workplace conflicts.

Explaining the finer points of InterArt's company policies is Chris Schrader's expertise.

> *While we are free to choose our actions, we are not free to choose the consequence of our actions.*
>
> —Stephen R. Covey

Post-Viewing Questions

1. Name some typical company policies designed to resolve problems.

_____

_____

2. How can hiring policies affect the resolution of workplace problems?

_____

_____

3. Why are formal policies and rules important?

_____

_____

Out of the Picture

When Wynfred returned from maternity leave, she hung a picture of her new baby on the wall in front of her desk. Within a month, John hung a picture of his three children above his desk. Martha didn't have children, so she hung up a picture of her dog.

Within the next six months, Jamila had added a picture of her car; Javier had added pictures of his extended family; Mikal, a picture of Jesus; and Akira hung up his favorite joke.

The look of the large office had gone from a clean, professional atmosphere to a diverse family album. Miranda, the office manager, was concerned about the upcoming visit from the corporate office. How would they feel about the addition of these personal pieces of art?

Miranda decided to talk to Ben, the service operations manager, about her concerns. "How do you think the corporate office will feel about all of the pictures?" Miranda asked.

"I can't imagine they will like it," Ben responded. "They've spent a lot of money decorating the office, complete with artwork. I don't believe they want their look changed with people's family pictures," Ben responded.

"What should I do?" Miranda bemoaned.

"Just tell everyone to take their photographs down," Ben said matter-of-factly.

"I think they'll be upset. These pictures are important to them," Miranda sighed. "I'll have to think of something soon, the corporate office is coming in one week."

 What should Miranda do? What experiences have you encountered concerning policies and personal belongings in your workplace? With a partner, write a company policy concerning personal workspace. Be prepared to share it with the class.

_____

_____

_____

_____

> *Good management is the art of making problems so interesting and their solutions so constructive that everyone wants to get to work and deal with them.*
>
> —Paul Hawken

PRACTICE

1. With a small group, chose a small, local employer (one that you're familiar with) and create a set of policies for that company. Justify the need for each policy. Display your policies in a two-column report. The left column header should be "Policy," and the right column "Justification." Share your policies with the class.

2. Using your two-column reports from Practice #1, make a chart noting the similarities between each group's list of company policies. Discuss the similarities and the differences.

3. With a partner, role-play a disciplinary meeting for a policy violation. Each team should share a different section of the procedure and discuss how it felt to be either the "enforcer" of a policy or the disciplined employee. Offer constructive comments for providing effective, non-threatening discipline. Consult previous workshops for assistance.

4. Using the Internet or other sources, find at least two company policies and compare the policies about absenteeism and dress codes. Develop a brief report contrasting the policies, how they may be justified, and how violations are handled.

SUMMARY

➤ A company's disciplinary action policy can be the best point of reference when problems arise.

➤ Company policies are created to serve as control devices for standards of behavior.

➤ Just as organizations require rules to operate, employees require information about those rules and an understanding of the consequences of violating them.

➤ Disciplinary policies generally allow enough time for employees to make necessary adjustments to workplace behaviors.

➤ Many businesses find that the use of progressive discipline is effective for producing positive outcomes.

1. Why are company policies important to an organization?

_____

_____

_____

2. Why should terms such as "excessive tardiness" or "repeated absences" be defined in a handbook?

_____

_____

_____

3. List a possible four-step sequence of disciplinary progression.

_____

_____

_____

4. List at least three company policies that are intended to avert problems. Would violations of these policies typically be subject to termination or to warning?

_____

_____

_____

DID YOU KNOW?

According to a recent American Management Association survey, nearly 80% of major U.S. companies keep tabs on employees by checking their e-mail, Internet, or phone connections, or by videotaping them at work.

More than a quarter of surveyed companies (27%) say that they've fired employees for misuse of office e-mail or Internet connections, and nearly two-thirds (65%) reported some disciplinary measure for those offenses.

1. Visit two to three companies in your community and ask for copies of their employee handbooks. (You may have to settle for a copy of their company policies, but explain in detail how you plan to use the handbook.) Compare and contrast the policies and determine how the businesses justify those policies in a two- to three-column document.

2. Using community newspapers, Internet news sources, magazines, and television, compile a selection of at least six stories that exemplify policy breaking and the disciplinary action that resulted. Develop a summary of your findings.

A company's disciplinary action policy can be the best point of reference when problems arise.

©2001 PhotoDisc, Inc.

On the Net

Created in 1971, the Occupational Safety & Health Administration (OSHA) works within the U.S. Department of Labor and is charged with assuring safe and healthy conditions for working men and women. Today, 105 million private-sector workers and employers at nearly 7 million work sites rely on OSHA to set and enforce workplace health and safety standards. To learn more about this important government agency, go to:

www.osha.gov

81

FIELD STUDY

This guide has presented various effective strategies for solving problems and conflicts. In teams of three, use what you've learned to develop a presentation entitled "Conflict Resolution." Each team will need to create a one-hour presentation on three key concepts from this guide. Presentations will include handouts and activities. After the presentation, each team member should submit a self-evaluation. Your instructor will select portions of your finished workshop to present to the class.

When planning your presentation, be sure to consider the following elements.

Topic
Select topics that your group feels are vital to teaching conflict resolution skills.

Content
The information presented should be accurate and detailed. Sources should be cited. Include information from this guide and at least two alternate sources, such as the Internet magazines, or books.

Visuals
Use visuals or teaching aids to enhance the presentation, such as posters, overheads, or PowerPoint slides.

Handouts
Handouts can serve as an information source or as aids for note-taking during the presentation. They can take many forms, such as brochures, articles, outlines, or worksheets.

Activity
Activities should be used to involve the audience and can include the entire class or a select group for the class to observe. They can be role-plays, skill practice, brainstorming, group discussions, or other appropriate activities.

Questions and Answers
Encourage participants to question and clarify new concepts. In case there are no questions from the group, create some questions you can ask them to check for comprehension of the material.

PRESENTATION WORKSHEET 1

Topic 1: _____

_____

Content: _____

_____

_____

_____

_____

_____

Visuals: _____

_____

_____

_____

Handouts: _____

_____

_____

_____

Activity: _____

_____

_____

_____

Questions and Answers: _____

_____

_____

_____

PRESENTATION WORKSHEET 2

Topic 2: _____

_____

Content: _____

_____

_____

_____

_____

_____

Visuals: _____

_____

_____

_____

Handouts: _____

_____

_____

_____

Activity: _____

_____

_____

_____

Questions and Answers: _____

_____

_____

_____

PRESENTATION WORKSHEET 3

Topic 3: _____

_____

Content: _____

_____

_____

_____

_____

_____

Visuals: _____

_____

_____

_____

Handouts: _____

_____

_____

_____

Activity: _____

_____

_____

_____

Questions and Answers: _____

_____

_____

_____

GLOSSARY

A

accountability—taking responsibility for your choices and their results

active listening—the act of playing an active role in the listening process, which includes questioning and clarifying information

advice—counsel or suggestion as to a course of action

arbitration—the process of settling a dispute between two or more parties by an unbiased third party

arbitrator—a person or team who is empowered to make a judgment in a mediation case

B

belief—a conviction that certain things are true or real; confidence; faith; trust; an opinion

binding arbitration—an arbitration decision of a neutral third party that all parties in a dispute agree to accept

brainstorming—the unrestrained suggestion of ideas on a topic

C

conflict—a sharp disagreement over interests or ideas

criticism—severe judgment or censure

D

decision—something that is chosen or determined after considering possible alternatives

disciplinary action—penalty or punishment associated with violation of a rule

E

empathy—the ability to identify with and understand another person's feelings or difficulties

F

fair—just; honest

I

interest—a true want or attraction

L

listening—making a conscious effort to hear; paying close attention to what others are saying

M

mediator—an impartial person or team that comes in when two quarreling parties formally agree to have a third party help to resolve the conflict

N

negotiation—the process of attempting to resolve differences in order to reach agreements

netiquette—network etiquette, the correct way to conduct yourself when you're communicating online or on a computer network

nonverbal behavior—methods of communicating without spoken language

P

perspective—a particular evaluation of a situation or facts, especially from one person's point of view

policy—a pre-established regulation for dealing with an issue or a problem

probation—trial period during which a worker is given time to correct performance problems

position—a policy, view, or opinion, especially an official one

proactive—taking the initiative by acting rather than reacting to events

problem—a difficult situation, matter, or person; a question or puzzle that needs to be solved

R

reactive—reacting to events, situations, and stimuli, especially doing so spontaneously as they occur

S

speaking to share—projecting an open, approachable listening style

standard—something established for use as a rule or basis of comparison in measuring or judging fairness

stress—mental or physical tension or strain

symptom—an indication of a disorder or problem

U

underlying interests—issues or situations that drive bargaining positions

understanding—knowing or grasping what is meant; interpreting; having a thorough comprehension of a subject

W

worldview—a personal interpretation or image of the universe and humanity; view of life